Awakened
Instincts

Awakened Instincts

Seven Keys for Enhancing Every Aspect of Your Life

MARYROSE OCCHINO

with Jacqueline Sullivan

ATRIA BOOKS

New York   London   Toronto   Sydney

ATRIA BOOKS

A Division of Simon & Schuster, Inc.
1230 Avenue of the Americas
New York, NY 10020

First Atria Books hardcover edition April 2008

ATRIA BOOKS and colophon are trademarks of Simon & Schuster, Inc.

For information about special discounts for bulk purchases, please contact Simon & Schuster Special Sales at 1-800-456-6798 or business@simonandschuster.com.

Designed by Dana Sloan

Manufactured in the United States of America

10 9 8 7 6 5 4 3 2 1

Library of Congress Cataloging-in-Publication Data

Occhino, MaryRose.
    Awakened instincts : seven keys for enhancing every aspect of your life / by MaryRose Occhino with Jacqueline Sullivan.
        p. cm.
    Includes bibliographical references and index.
    1. Success. 2. Psychic energy (Psychoanalysis). 3. Psychic ability. 4. Intuition. I. Sullivan, Jacqueline Levering. II. Title.

BF637.S8023 2008
158.1—dc22   2007040256

ISBN-13: 978-1-4767-6249-4

For Aunt Sadie (Maggie Errico),
who always believed my and Jacqueline's
intuitive gift was special and is now
our special angel in heaven.

For my cousin, Cathy Errico,
· who left our physical plane much too soon,
but is teaching us even as we write this dedication
just how precious our physical life is.

Contents

Introduction

Once upon a time not so long ago lived a woman named Mary whose life was less than perfect, but profound nonetheless. Mary was divorced and had three children—two grown sons, Chris, twenty-five, and Carl, twenty-three, and her youngest, daughter Jacqueline, who was only ten years old.

Mary's sons were young adults and independent, leaving Mary and Jacqueline to depend on each other. Mary and her daughter, Jacqueline, developed a special bond, becoming as close as a mother and daughter could be. While there's nothing extraordinary about a single mother developing a special connection with her only daughter, the union between Mary and Jacqueline was anything but ordinary.

People who knew them said they were as close as two peas in a pod. In fact, the energy between them was so intense when they were together that they seemed literally to be feeding off of one another's life-force.

Mary and Jacqueline shared such an instinctive link with each other that whenever they were in a room it seemed brighter. One could feel a heartwarming sense of positive energy radiating between them. But thir bright optimistic essence was about to become dimmed. In a blink of an eye, when they least expected it, a life-changing event happened.

Mary and Jacqueline's brilliant force faded almost into complete darkness. It was as if someone had turned off the electricity that had surrounded them so effortlessly. But Mary and Jacqueline, never quick to surrender, worked together to find the switch that would turn their magnetic light back on. And this time, when their instincts reunited and they entered a room, it wasn't just a shimmering glow that surrounded them, but rather an explosion of fireworks.

We invite you to accompany Mary and Jacqueline on their journey from their darkest hours to their renewed star-lite auras. As you read on, you'll experience their miracles of positive energy and the enlightenment of their instincts against what seemed to be insurmountable odds.

Awakened Instincts is their guide to illumination and conscious awakened instincts that they want to share with you. It's no coincidence that you have found this book, or that this book has found you. Take this as a sign from the universe, and from those who guide you, that this book didn't just accidentally fall into your hands. It was put there as a signal from your subconscious, which has received an answer to its pleas for a better life.

Unseen energies have come to your rescue and will show you what you must do in order to enhance every aspect of your life, something which most of humanity has been trying to do since the invention of the wheel. But you don't need a new invention to enhance your life. All you need is a little spiritual nudge to point you in the right direction. You can consider this book your spiritual nudge.

As you read on, remember, as Mary and Jacqueline have, to follow your God-given instincts. Listen, and observe the directions you will be receiving during your life's journey. Pursue your desires with a passion and don't allow your instincts to doze ever again, not even for a moment. Then you will find that you, too, can awaken your instincts and, in so doing, create and enhance the life you have dreamed of having. Welcome to your new and improved life. Enjoy your journey as Mary and Jacqueline are enjoying theirs!

Awakened Instincts

Some Things Lost
Can Be Found

Although I believe I've been psychic since birth and I've been very much in tune with the energy around me, I can honestly say that there was a time in my life, especially after I was diagnosed with multiple sclerosis, that I somehow unknowingly closed the intuitive gate to my instincts. Once that gate closed, I needed to find new keys to reopen the gate and keep it open for good.

Living an intuitive awakened life was the only kind of life I had ever known. Fortunately, my instincts weren't lost forever. They were simply misplaced somewhere, deep inside what had become my hazy psyche. In hindsight, I realize that my perceptive vision wasn't blocked because I had somehow become less intuitive or because of my newly diagnosed disability. It was because my gut instincts drifted off to an unknown place, somewhere very much like a deserted island. My instincts were blinded because I was missing my "third eye."

Our Third Eye

My third eye, also known as the astral eye, was nowhere to be found. I looked and looked for my third eye, but I kept coming up empty.

I know many of you reading this may have heard the term third eye with respect to psychic intuition. Some of you are probably staring blankly at this page, thinking, "What the heck is she talking about? A third eye?" Allow me to explain.

An encyclopedia definition of the third eye is a metaphysical and esoteric concept referring to the anja chakra, located at our brow. (Chakra is a Sanskrit term that expresses the life-force energy in our body. We have chakras located all over our bodies. The sixth chakra, situated at the brow, or the lower forehead between the eyes, is also known as the third eye. I explain chakras and their significance in great detail in the chapter on telepathy.)

The third eye goes far beyond a simple dictionary definition. It is also known as a symbol of enlightenment, especially associated with visions, clairvoyance, and precognitions. It allows us to see and feel with our soul and inner core. In my case, my third eye has made me extremely sensitive and conscious of the world and the energies around me. (Keep in mind some people work a lifetime to develop this level of ability with their third eye.)

Additionally, my third eye has enlightened me with information that has helped me emotionally. It enabled me instinctively to understand more about my illness, and all illnesses, as time went by. I was able to see what would help or hinder me. My third eye helps me with anything that may pertain to my life or my well-being, or the well-being of others.

Reaching Your Personal Universe

My third eye allows me to access my personal universe. This is the place where my soul exists. My personal universe is the place where all my reasons for living and being are kept.

Your personal universe is not a secret place, but a place all your own. It's as unique as your DNA. In fact, when you visit your personal universe, it's as though you're getting reacquainted with your DNA—your reasoning and your purpose in life. It belongs to no one but you.

It's natural to doubt that you have a personal universe and a third eye. But even if you're not aware of those very special parts of you, they're there, and I'm going to show you how to find them.

I know the terms personal universe and third eye may seem odd to you. Well, third-eye terminology isn't my creation—it's been around for thousands of years. The personal universe expression is my own premise, but it's simple enough that even paranormal skeptics should find it easy to swallow. In case you're still having a little trouble, here's a scenario that may help you to understand the everyday uses of your third eye and your personal universe. (It's of paramount importance to me that this book be easy for novices of psychic phenomena to understand. No offense to those who hold PhDs in quantum physics, but there's no big scientific brain needed to follow these uncomplicated lessons.)

You've probably heard someone referred to as "living in her own world." You know the kind of person I'm speaking about—the one who seems to be drifting off into space, not paying attention to the world around her, with her mind up in the clouds. When we think of the phrase, "living in your own world," it usually carries a negative connotation, as if the person we're talking about is a bit loony, out there, or just a smidge gaga. To tell you the truth, even now, when I think about how I have used the phrase, it sounds kind of freaky to me, too. But I do believe that living in your own world, at times, can be a very good thing—as long as it's done for the right reasons, and as long as you don't stay away from reality for too long.

"Being a little spacey," to me, means getting away from others for awhile and being silently by yourself. It's a way to help yourself zero in on your own wellness. Now, some people believe that just being alone, away from others, allows them to become centered again when they're feeling uncentered, even if they're still communicating with the outside world via telephone or email. Well, I've got news for you: as far as I'm concerned, no can do! You've got to be alone-alone. Really alone, with no outside suggestions or opinions, and that means no television or radio, either. Everyone and everything has to get shut out. Don't get yourself in a panic. You won't have to "be a little spacey" for very long. Just long enough for you to see yourself for what you're worth—not in material value or monetary value, but in a spiritual and intuitive sense.

While we're "spacing out," what we're really doing is looking inside ourselves at the very real issues that are going on in our lives, with spot-on objectivity and without being influenced by the opinions of others. We're living, and dealing with, our own reality. It's what some people call finding their center or looking inward.

Before you go any further into these lessons, you must understand that you cannot enhance your life or boost any aspect of it with the overindulgence of drugs or alcohol. Our job in this life is to remember why we were put on this earth—something that can only be understood when our minds are clear of mind-altering substances. I believe we are here with the object of finally "getting it," remembering why we are here and what path we hope to be on.

And please keep in mind—we all have different paths and different wants and we can't shove our desires into someone else's life journey. That would be like trying to fit a square peg into a round hole. And we all know that just doesn't work.

Using Your Personal Universe

There are occasions when I find it necessary to drift off by myself and find my center. Those instances come around because I may have gotten caught up in the whirlwind of life.

You may find yourself off course for many reasons. Perhaps you have simply too much stress in your life. Or you may be recovering from a bad flu and you physically feel out of sorts. Or maybe you've just ended a relationship with someone you thought was Mr. or Ms. Right.

Whatever the reason, you need to get back and find your center—to remember why you are here. It's like rediscovering the reasons for your existence. You can recall how to enjoy your life, and how to love the life and the physical body you're occupying. Finding your center, or becoming centered again, feels as though you've found a magical spiritual prescription that works as an antibiotic for your soul. (A prescription, I am certain, that isn't covered by any HMO!)

For example, I used to get caught up in other people's energy and distracted from my path. (Thank God I'm now mentally signaled by my subconscious, which in turn awakens my consciousness, so I'm aware of when I'm getting caught up in other people's energy before it's too late.) Sometimes my head is just spinning from having put too many demands upon myself—a feeling I'm sure you've also had more than once. On those occasions, I go into deep thought and meditate in my own personal world where no one knows me like I know me. The trick, then, is to find me again before I get lost in the crowd of the universe's energy. So I pull back and visit my personal universe.

Sometimes this happens spontaneously; sometimes you have to concentrate to do it. I've now trained myself and my consciousness to know when I need to get back on track, so my mind automatically goes there without any outside coaxing. Other times I indeed schedule time with my subconscious—consciously—and take time out of my normal routine to find out what's really going on in my personal world.

So how can you "subconsciously" schedule time with yourself "consciously"? It's simple. All you have to do is to tell yourself that the next time you feel yourself going off base, you'd like to be reminded, or given a heads-up, when it's happening again. Your subconscious mind will then awaken your consciousness as to what's going on with you.

Looking into your personal universe helps you reconfigure your energy, just the same way you would reconfigure a computer that is moving too slowly or is frozen completely.

You know, when you think about it, we're really more like computers than we realize. We need to reboot our minds in order to awaken our instincts, the same way our computers need to be rebooted when they become frozen. I'm sure I don't have to remind you how you feel when your computer freezes up. It drives me to the brink of insanity sometimes, especially when I have a deadline and my computer refuses to respond to my commands. Well, when our instincts become frozen because of life's mishaps or because of stress-related overload, we need to use our very own virtual surge protector. That's our natural instincts, which can only be acquired in our personal universe.

How can closing off the rest of the world or going within ourselves awaken our instincts? Believe it or not, most of us do it all the time, but we're just unaware of it. When we go off into our own little world, or when we meditate and zero in on ourselves, it's a way for us to release our minds as well as our immune systems from the tensions or difficulties that we may be having. Think of yourself exploring your personal universe and finding the keys that open the door to relaxation for your soulful muscles. Consider it a visit to a spiritual day spa.

The time we spend in our personal universe is very important for our psychic intuition as well as our physical well-being. While we're in our zone, or what some of us call "zoning out," we get a chance to read and perceive the information the universe is sending us. This information will help us to comprehend the kinds of energy we're attracting from around us (energies emanating from certain people or situations), and give us a heads-up on what we should be doing about any negative or unhealthy vibrations that may be coming our way.

Losing My Sight—In More Ways Than One

At the time when my vision was temporarily blocked, my connection to my personal universe seemed to have vanished. My perception to the information the universe was sending me was gone, and my normally awakened instincts were void of thought.

I no longer had easy access to the adventurer in me. In the past, I was always able to search and investigate the energies of not only my surroundings, but of people and/or issues that were not in my physical presence at the time. This was my third eye.

My internal invisible gaze or my center eye had always worked almost like a superhero laser beam, honing in on targets. In some cases, this may have been reading someone's thoughts—what's commonly known as telepathy, or being telepathic. Also, I would often get a feeling about an outcome to a situation, therefore I was clairvoyant about many things that had not yet happened. I had come to rely on these special gifts, and now I realized I had taken these gifts for granted. The extraordinary enlightenments I was so accustomed to seemed to be hiding from me, somewhere far, far away in an unknown distant universe. I was desperate to find them and get them back.

I missed that part of me the same way someone would miss a limb. Without my intuitive awareness, I wasn't able to "see" the way I saw before. I felt crippled in more ways than one.

It was my awakened instincts that had allowed me to explore the consciousness and needs of my children, my friends, my family, and my careers, plus all of my personal relationships. And now they had somehow become numb.

That special intuitive element of my being—a bequest since birth— had become as anesthetized as one's gums after getting a Novocain injection for a root canal. And the reason for my inherent lapse was nothing other than two key components: shock and outrage.

I was shocked and outraged that God and the universe had dealt me such a rotten hand with my disease, multiple sclerosis. I couldn't comprehend, no matter how hard I tried, that my life, the life I had always known, the life of a mentally strong and physically independent single parent, was disappearing before my very eyes.

My vision problem was the first apparent symptom. It's what's commonly known among neurologists or MS specialists as optic neuritis, an inflammation behind the optic nerve. It's a common condition or symptom found in MS sufferers.

My sight was changing from one day to another. Some days I could see as well as I did before my new medical diagnosis. But most days when I awoke, I remember feeling as though my eyes had a layer of film on them. I had gotten into the habit of rubbing them in the first minutes after I awoke, trying to wipe off whatever seemed to be coating my eyes. When I saw friends and family, I would ask them, "Do you see anything in my eyes?" (I already had told them about my vision problems so they were happy to try to help me in any way they could.) I'd walk up close to the person I was questioning, nearly nose-to-nose, and hold my eyelid open so they could get a good look into my eyes. And after their careful examination of my pupils, their answers were always the same. "Mary, I don't see anything floating around in there anywhere."

But their inability to find a problem didn't satisfy my perplexed and frightened mind. In my heart of hearts, I knew they were probably right, but I wasn't ready to accept their answers. Why? Because if they were correct and there wasn't anything actually floating in my eyes, it meant I was really ill. MS was actually changing my nervous system and affecting my sight and that frightened me beyond words.

And so, I lived in my state of denial for as long as I could. I tried ignoring my medical condition as well as everyone's inability to find that floating object that was marring my vision. I continued to pray that one day someone would finally look inside my eyes and say, "Hey Mary, you know what? You're right, there is something floating around in there!" Boy, that answer would have made me one happy camper.

But soon after the first few times I questioned my friends or family about my eyes, I got tired of the subconscious game that I was playing with myself. I also tired of asking other people for their opinions about my life.

The exception was my daughter Jacqueline. Why, of all the people in my life, would I continue to ask Jacqueline, who was only ten years old at the time? The answer is simple. I knew Jacqueline wouldn't lie to me, and although my senses seemed to have gone askew, I still knew that my daughter knew me best—body, mind, and spirit—almost as well as I did. Or, the way I used to know me before I lost my relationship with my personal universe.

Fear Can Turn into a Chronic Disease

Jacqueline, or Jackie, as I often call her, could psychically as well as telepathically read me. Sometimes her telepathy was a gift, and other times a burden—it all depended on the way we looked at it on any given day.

If I was feeling well, I didn't mind Jackie being able to read my feelings and thoughts. But if I wasn't feeling well, I would try to shut her out of my vibratory energy. Try as I might, Jackie could always break through. She inherited her instincts from me, as I believe I inherited mine from the women in our family.

Not only was my eyesight in trouble, I had also lost the intuitive link to my consciousness which had always connected me to the energies around me. I found myself needing Jackie's input more than ever before. This was the new Mary, the one who could no longer rely on her intuitive third eye. How could this happen?

Here's how. In the physical body, the eye views objects upside-down. It sends the image of what it observes to the brain, which interprets the image and makes it appear right side up. The human body has another eye—the third eye—which in reality is the pineal gland. The pineal gland is not an actual eye, but is believed by some to be a dormant organ that can be awakened to enable telepathic communication.

So you could say my chakras were asleep. I was having trouble seeing with my two natural eyes, and also struggling to connect with my telepathic and psychic communicator. In essence, I was forgetting what it was to be me, the person who once lived inside my head. The person who knew what was happening to her life with regard to the past, present, and the future.

But poor Jackie. There were times that she couldn't get away from my questions, even if she wanted to. You see, even if I didn't ask her any questions out loud, she was still telepathic. She could usually sense what I was feeling, especially during those times I was upset. Because we shared the same bedroom, she was right there when I woke up every morning and she was there to witness my daily eye-rubbing ritual. She realized what I was doing without me saying one word.

Now as I look back on how fast she had to grow up, especially when dealing with my illness, I'm saddened. The tides of our lives were turning way too quickly, with Jackie having to be my sometimes-caretaker instead of me being hers. This would begin once she walked in the door, coming home from play or school. Jackie could no longer be a little girl living in a fantasy world of Barbie dolls and dress-up. No, once she opened our apartment door Jackie became my health partner in the fight of my life. She helped not only as my life preserver, but also by helping me stay afloat mentally, stopping me from drowning in deep despair.

As I think back now on those times, I'm very proud of how caring and extremely intuitive she was at such a young age. She continues to be that way today.

Jackie knew just how to handle me. Every time I think about how mature she was, it blows my mind. In hindsight, I realize that my own fears may have become intertwined in her own consciousness and that saddens me all the more. If I could turn back time, if I could have just one wish, it would be that Jackie hadn't had to grow up so quickly, leaving her childhood securities behind at all too early an age. You know the securities I'm talking about—the ones most of us enjoyed when we were kids. "Don't worry. Mommy will take care of everything."

But our cards weren't dealt that way. Jackie unfortunately experienced through her subconscious every symptom I had. She felt and heard my rants, my cries, and sometimes my laughter when I couldn't figure out what the heck was going to happen to my body or to my mind next.

Jackie was there with me as my fears grew. When monstrously, my fears grew way out of proportion or I seemed to be physically crashing, Jackie would always remind me of my strengths. She helped keep me from caving in to my fears and at those times she would become my little cheerleader. One of her favorite cheers was, "Mom, you have to fight this thing." She would say this with such conviction that she'd make me remember that I was in charge of my own body. Jackie's cheer made me remember the strong-willed Mary that had lived through many different disappointments and illnesses. Such as a sudden hysterectomy at thirty-one, emergency back surgery, and a long list of other ailments I believe were brought on by stress. So with Jackie's positive voice ringing in my ear, I started to believe that even though I maybe couldn't cure this disease, I sure wasn't going to get comfortable living with it. I was going to fight it—for her and for me.

Jackie is more than just my daughter. She is an extension of my consciousness, and she's been at my side every step of the way. From the minute I would wake up in the morning until I'd lay my head down to sleep, Jackie was there for me. Still, now, she's here for me and I am forever grateful to God and the universe for sending her to me.

But back then, I shared a little one-bedroom garden apartment on Long Island, New York, with my daughter. I would wake up every morning rubbing my eyes, trying to shake off my blurry vision. Before long, I realized my eyes weren't sleepy or hazy, but just sick. And so, I had to come to grips with my fears and the reality that I had MS. For all the rubbing I would do, I couldn't wake up or erase the large white spider-shaped film that impaired my vision in the bright sunlight. Nor could I erase the black floating spots that appeared whenever I looked or focused on anything bright, like the walls of my bedroom or the morning sunshine.

The sun only made my vision worse. Ironically, one of the main reasons I was so excited about renting our new apartment was that it was on the sunny side of the street. Now my bedroom's beautiful bay window was a constant reminder that I was ill, and the morning's light was the most depressing part of my day. Those mornings made me realize that this thing, MS, the condition that the doctors had diagnosed me with, wasn't going away—not yet anyway. That ticked me off and made me fearful. And, dear readers, fear is an illness all its own.

After intense soul searching and with help from my daughter Jackie, I finally confronted my fears and realized that I didn't like the way I was reacting to these unwanted parts of my new life. I realized I was becoming an anxious, frightened wreck who was manifesting every negative emotion I could conjure in my frightened fearful mind.

What was I afraid of? I was afraid of the unknown and every danger that might be lying ahead of me. I realized that I was becoming more and more fearful of life, and I didn't know this fearful person. This Mary was a total stranger to me and so were these fears. Fears were locking many of the doors to my instincts.

Not all of my instincts were closed for business. If I needed to, I could still read other people and answer questions about their lives as long as they had nothing to do with me. But when it came to my own life, I literally and metaphorically couldn't see my own way out of a paper bag.

Most people (but not Jacqueline) believed I was fearless. They thought I would and could overcome anything that the universe could throw at me, but I was frightened out of my mind.

And you know what happens when you're afraid of what's coming next? That something comes next!

One day when I awoke and rubbed my eyes the way I had done on so many previous mornings, for once there were no floaters in my left eye. You'd think I'd be thrilled to be rid of them, finally, but no. Why? Because that morning I was totally blind in that eye. Thank goodness I could still see the floaters in my right eye, so I hadn't completely lost my physical vision. Then I realized how much I suddenly missed the once-annoying floating spots in my left eye.

I was lucky. The loss of sight in my left eye lasted for only seven weeks. My doctors told me the optic neuritis I was suffering was a common occurrence with MS patients. It didn't feel common to me, and those seven weeks felt like an eternity. The doctors were quick to warn me that there was no guarantee that my vision would ever come back.

Interestingly, that's the exact time my then ten-year-old daughter Jackie became my assistant, both spiritually and scientifically. Jackie, being an intuitive by nature and also sharing my zodiac sign, Scorpio, was quick to tell me when I was being too whiny. She gave me the courage and the tools to find my own way back to me—the tough, fearless mother she had once known.

Once the shock of my blindness wore off and I had a chance to meditate and really sit down with my feelings, I started to ask myself some tough questions. The big question: did my fear of losing my sight make me lose my sight?

When I asked myself that question I considered that my anxieties most definitely added to my condition. To make sure I wasn't all to blame, I asked my doctors and they said it was just a symptom of MS. But as they said those words, my heart and my intuition told me that I had truly made my fears become my reality.

And as the years went on, I became whole again, not just like before, but I was a better Mary than before. My daughter became a better Jacqueline than before by utilizing her intuition while helping me rediscover mine. I knew I had to write this book, with my daughter's help, because Jackie and I learned so many lessons along the way. The lessons changed us in every aspect of our lives, and we want to and need to share them with you. My friends, we call these lessons, "The Seven Keys to Enhance Every Aspect of Your Life."

The Seven Keys to Enhance Your Life

1. Fearlessness
2. Expect the unexpected (miracles)
3. Arise to every occasion
4. Relax your energy
5. Never say never!
6. Observe
7. Telepathy

Now, if you've already discovered the acronym found in the seven aspects to enhance your life, bravo! If you haven't, don't feel bad. It took me a while to hear and observe what my guides wanted me to get across to you, and that's FEARNOT. That's what is spelled out, when you list these aspects. Keep in mind this book is not a test, but a guide to help you enhance your life in every aspect, as it has for my daughter and myself. An extra benefit is that you'll become FEARLESS in the process, too!

To get you started straight away on developing your instincts for your own life enhancements, I'd like for us to establish an introduction to each other. Through this telepathic exploring of each other's consciousness, we will start a friendship. The words and intentions as well as affirmations you are about to read come from my heart and soul. I share them with you, and I want for you all that I want for myself.

Before we begin learning about our first key, I'd like to get your engines roaring and give you eleven positive affirmations to say to yourself, out loud if possible. So my dear new friend, imagine you and I are sitting on my living room couch, and I've just handed you my private diary. You're reading it out loud for me and for you our positive affirmations and declarations.

We are declaring the way the world will see us and how we will see and be greeted by the universe. My daughter and I have tested these affirmations/declarations and so far so good. I take that back. So far, so great!

Your Fearless Declarations

1. My life's energy will be enhanced immediately and it will withdraw from its limbo state-of-being. Everything that I've been waiting for will start manifesting exactly the way I've dreamed and visualized it—beginning today!

2. I can see the image of the new and improved me as I look within the mirror of my soul. My new awakened life begins right now.

3. I am sufficient enough to accomplish all my desires just the way I am.

4. I will stop being afraid of the unknown and I will close the door to my past mistakes and hurts.

5. I am happily anticipating my bright future.

6. I am in the process of developing my individual power and I will search deep inside myself in order to own my unique characteristics, and reveal the identity of my emotional consciousness and intuition.

7. It's time I become healthier and understand that I'm entering a healing journey that will keep my vibratory (energy) levels balanced.

8. I will challenge my mind and body both mentally and physically without doing harm to myself.

9. I will rid myself of all bad and unhealthy habits that I've been holding on to for much too long.

10. I will set goals for myself that I will achieve with ease.

11. I will not allow myself to live by anyone else's life standards. I am the master of my universe!

Now that you've declared your affirmations to the universe for the new and enhanced you, you're ready to move on to the next level. Welcome to our world, and enjoy your journey.

Every Step Brings You Closer to Perfection!

On our journey to find your keys, we first need to work on the inner you. Together, let's travel into your subconscious, learn to relax your mind, and find strength to change the parts of you that you're not happy with. I know many of you may not be certain of what is causing you to feel unhappy. I'm certain, however, that you've been receiving more than a few hints from the universe about what is not quite right with your inner core. Those hints are there inside you just waiting for you to shake them awake so that you can become the most perfect you.

If you believe you're just fine the way you are, and you've convinced yourself that you can handle your life as you've been doing all these years without someone helping you or directing you to a new and improved life-path, good for you. But if you're reading this page at this very moment, I'd say the universe believes differently. You see, the universe wants you to realize that we can always learn new things and new ways of bettering our lives. Believe me, no matter how righteous we think we are and how well we believe we have a handle on our lives, there isn't a person alive who hasn't been spiritually deficient at one time or another. Do I believe that after you've awakened your instincts that you'll be absolutely perfect in life? No, I don't believe that anyone will ever be absolutely perfect in this life. To be honest, I wouldn't want to be. Think about it. If we were all perfect, there wouldn't be any more life journeys to learn by. But the one thing we do need to perfect is how we deal with our fears and anxieties. As with anything else in life, the choice is yours, and you need to be willing to carefully examine the nervousness, the worries and the fears that have plagued you. Get ready to kiss them all goodbye!

Step 1—Imagery

I'd like you to begin by imagining that your brain, which includes your subconscious and your fears, is like an onion.

No, I don't want you to think your brain has a sharp stinky odor that makes your eyes water. I want you to imagine your brain is a large healthy sweet onion with many layers.

Next, I'd like you to imagine that you're peeling away layers of the onion (your past and your subconscious). With each layer you strip off, you are delving deeper into your fears. But you're not going to just peel off a layer and throw it away. We're going to put those layers in a bowl of water to make a nice soup when you're done. But before we do, we're going to take a good look at those pungent onion layers of fears.

You see, I don't want you to just throw those fears away either. I want you to look at them, embrace them, learn from them, and realize that with each fear there was a journey. With every journey there was a learning experience that your soul needed to go through.

As we all know, everything happens to us for a reason. Whatever difficulties we've had at various times in our lives were necessary for our spiritual growth. To dispose of a layer of onion would be to throw away a part of our life journey. Even if that journey was one marred by fear, just discarding it would be a waste of time and emotions. If we disregard just one voyage, then I'm sorry to tell you that we may have to revisit that same hurt again, and I know we don't want to do that. So I'd like you to see your present fears as the first layer of your onion. Put it in a pot of water as part of the virtual broth that you'll be adding to with each layer of fear you come across.

When peeling off the layers of your onion do so very gently and with great care, because what you're actually doing is peeling off layers of your subconscious. With that in mind, be ever so careful not to injure your onion or the healthy, fearless part of your brain.

As you probe your subconscious, I'd like you to try to zone in on your fears and take a long hard look at them. Don't leave any of them out. Though it may be a difficult task, feel your fears and experience them. Try to remember when and where they all started. That first layer is your present fears, and the more layers you peel off, the deeper you will delve into your subconscious.

Your next step is to create a list in your mind. Something very much like a grocery shopping list, except this is a list of your fears, anxieties, and insecurities.

Now crease your imaginary list, making four folds. I'm asking you to fold it closed because even though this list is only written in your mind's eye, I want you to feel totally reassured that no one has access to your list of fears other than you.

Next, I'd like to you to virtually store your folded list safely away in a corner of your brain that you're not using at the moment.

Which part of your brain, you wonder? Trust me, there's plenty of room. The fact is we only use five percent of our brain, so there's plenty of open real estate for your fears and anxieties to lay low.

I don't have to be an intuitive to know that some of you who are reading this are having major anxiety attacks at the mere thought of revisiting your fears. And I'm just as certain that some of you are having brain cramps at the thought. I promise you that it will all be worth the effort, and once you really get started, it really won't be that hard. Keep in mind that each step brings you closer to the keys of changing your life for the better, permanently.

Step 2—Blocking Out the Outside World—Fearlessly!

Now I'd like you to imagine that your eyes are closed. That's right, I said only imagine them closed. Why only *imagine* them closed? Because if you don't keep your eyes open, you wouldn't be able to continue reading! (Just a little psychic humor . . .) OK, I'm just joking with you, but it's really necessary for you to imagine your eyes closed for this exercise. I want you to become accustomed to using your imagination and visualizing with ease before we go any deeper into our mental exercises.

With your eyes now virtually closed, I'd like you to imagine that you are purposely and consciously relaxing all the hectic, loud, negative and dramatic energy surrounding you. Unfortunately for all of us, there's usually plenty of those energies to go around. If you need some assistance to get you started, here's an example you can begin with.

Imagine that your next-door neighbor has his stereo blasting at top volume while you're trying to get some sleep. It's already midnight and you have to get up for work in five hours and you need your rest. Imagine that you first try to put your pillows around your ears to close out the noise, but alas, the music is too loud and it's not working.

Now, you're going to practice using your imagination, and even more importantly, you're going to practice becoming fearless. How? By seeing yourself as fearless.

If you're naturally timid, probably the last thing you would ever do would be to knock on your neighbor's door to ask them to turn down their loud music, for fear of an argument, or for fear they wouldn't like you anymore. Before today, you may have gone without those needed hours of sleep rather than confront that noisy, inconsiderate neighbor. Well, it's time for a change.

Imagine now that you're one tough cookie—not an aggressive person, but not a pushover, either. Rewire your mind with visions of a fearless person—one who's not afraid to voice your opinion, without negativity or violence. Imagine this new, confident and brave person is you. Remember that just because two people have conflicting ideas or principles, it doesn't mean they have to have an argument or a disagreement over it. Contrary thoughts are just independent thoughts, and if you approach a person with calmness in your thoughts and security in your voice, you have nothing to fear. When you feel the need to speak up for yourself, approach the subject peacefully.

As you get better at using your imagination and you grow more familiar with each step, you can make up your own scenarios. And once you've learned all the lessons of how to find the keys, you won't need to imagine any longer. All the lessons will translate into steps that will come to you naturally.

Step 3—Relax!

If you're still finding it hard to block out your fears and the outside world, try this next exercise—relaxing.

One way to relax the energy surrounding you is by picturing yourself floating on your back in a pool filled with cool, clean water, and without a care in the world. The air temperature is not too hot or too cold. There's just the slightest balmy breeze crossing your face and you're enjoying the peace and tranquility of the day. In the background you hear ever so quietly the chirping of baby bluebirds. Their melodic songs remind you that you are safe and at peace. (You may have to practice this exercise more than once, but not much more.)

Now that you've controlled and relaxed your surrounding energy, I'd like you to turn your attention to those fears that we were talking about, the ones you tucked in the corner of your brain. Think of your safe place as an invisible closet in your mind, where your list of fears is locked inside, out of reach. Now take that list out of its closet and give each of your fears and concerns a closer look. It's time to discover the real reasons for them.

Don't be afraid to uncover your fears. They can't hurt you. You are safe from your fears and you're finally taking total control of your life. Remember, you're floating in a beautiful pool of water on a sun-filled day without a care or a fear in the world. And now that you're not afraid to see what's been intruding on your peace of mind, you can react the way you were always meant to with regard to outside influences such as relationships, family, friends, careers, and anything else you can think of—but this time without any anxieties.

If you haven't prepared your list yet, let's take a break. I strongly recommend that you go back to the beginning and don't read on any further until you have completed at least a good chunk of your list. This is important because I really want you to understand your fears once and for all. I don't want you to read the words I've written just for the sake of reading yet another self-help book, because if you do, you'll just be wasting your time. I've been known to say, "This life is not a dress rehearsal!" So let's make this time count. Don't procrastinate or choose to say, "Oh, I'll make the list later," or, "Oh, I'll fix my life later." You know why? This *is* later.

If you have looked at your list and have established what you believe to be your major fears and trepidations, I'd like you to ask yourself this one simple question: "Why am allowing these fears to plague me?"

As an intuitive, I know what you're thinking at this very moment. You're thinking, "This is too hard and too complicated. I don't have the time, nor do I have the insight to know what my fears are. I'm not a psychiatrist!"

Relax. You don't need a doctorate to search inside your mind, soul, consciousness, or subconscious. All you need are the keys that I will give you. And once you learn how to find the keys, ah, that's when life becomes fun. Yes, I said fun. You know why? Because when you have all the keys you need to enjoy life, and you open all the doors to the happiness that was meant for you, you'll have a ball! The seven keys to enhancing your life will give you the courage to open the doors to your mind and your universe. You'll have the ability to close off the darkened corridors of doubt you once had.

Step 4—The Collective Unconscious and the Personal Unconscious

After you're done searching the essence of your subconscious, the next step is to probe your collective unconscious.

What's your collective unconscious? Well, Wikpedia, the free online encyclopedia, defines collective unconscious as a term of analytical psychology originally coined by Carl Jung. The collective unconscious refers to the unconscious that is common to all human beings. It is the reservoir of our experiences as a species, a kind of knowledge we are all born with.

The collective unconscious is inherited, and it's inside each one of us, far from the external world, which Jung called the personal unconscious.

The personal unconscious is accrued from your own personal experiences, and those are different for everyone. Your fears are part of your personal unconscious. The reason you need to search, seek, rummage, and do whatever you have to do to delve deep inside your inner thoughts is because that's where most of your fears are hiding. No one person's traumas or anxieties are exactly like anyone else's. Our fears and the trepidation that stops us from being all we can be are unique and different for each of us. Never forget that although we are all human beings with feelings that get hurt, we also have different spiritual and physical gifts.

As an "intuitive explorer of consciousness," a title conferred on me by Dr. Deepak Chopra, I can feel that many of you reading this are wondering how all of our fears can be so different, especially when you know other people who have gone through many of the same hurts and disappointments as you have. Although their fears may sound the same, I guarantee you that each of our minds and souls reacts to each one of our fears differently. Our responses to our fears are as different and unique as our DNA.

But we all do have one thing in common. We all hide our fears and some of us have become masters at it.

Masters at hiding our fears? That's right. And why, you may ask, are we hiding them? Believe it or not, most of us have locked our fears away because we loathe looking at them head on. We have closed the door to them, very much like a child who shuts a closet door and pulls the sheets over her head as she lies in her darkened bedroom, afraid that the boogeyman may come popping out when she is fast asleep.

Well, there's no boogeyman here. I'd like you to pose the following questions to yourself, and then mentally respond with the answers I've stated here after the questions.

Question 1: "Am I ready to enjoy life without a fear in the world?"
Answer: "Yes, I am ready to enjoy my life without fear."

Question 2: "Am I entitled to a happy life?"
Answer: "I am more than entitled to a happy life. I expect a happy life!"

Question 3: "To become truly fearless, what would I change in my life?"
Answer: "I would change everything that made me insecure and anxious!"

Question 4: "After exploring and becoming mindful of my fears, would I end or begin a new relationship?"
Answer: This is one response you'll have to express based on

your current circumstances. While you're thinking about your answer to this question, keep in mind that most of us hang on to bad relationships because we're afraid of being alone. Or, we believe that we're just not good enough for anyone else. Once your fear is gone, you'll stand taller and look better than ever, with confidence to spare.

Question 5: "Have I had enough anxiety for one lifetime?"

Answer: "I've had enough anxiety for many lifetimes and enough is enough! I am strong now and I can handle any situation that comes my way!"

Question 6: "Do I want to pass on my fears to my family or my children?"

Answer: "I want my children and family to know that they can count on me to be a stable figure in their life."

Question 7: "Do I want to live in heaven or hell on earth?"

Answer: "Without fear in my life, every day will be heavenly! With fear in my life every day will be hellish."

These answers are just a starting point for you—some ideas for you to be thinking about and suggestions for the frame of mind you should be in.

On the blank lines provided in the next few pages, I'd like you to write your own answers. Start with question one. But don't just answer with a simple yes or no. Go into detail. Then I'd like you to go one step further and think about why you answered the question the way you did. A carefully crafted and understood answer written today means you'll have a great resource that you can go back to and reread later on if you feel yourself becoming fretful again. I found that looking back at the way I answered my questions helped remind me why I needed to explore my subconscious fears in the first place. Looking back at your responses will serve the same purpose for you.

In the pages that follow, you'll have room to answer each of the seven questions with space to spare. But while you're putting your answer and an explanation down, remember that no one is looking over your shoulder. These pages and this book belong to you and you alone, so your secrets are safe in your hands. One little interjection: don't share your journey of fears with anyone. Not your husband, or your wife, or your best friend, your co-worker, or your child. This is yours alone to look back on and to make peace with. What we're trying to do is remember, then let go. If you show someone your most inner fears, it can make you very vulnerable to someone someday. Your fears could be thrown back in your face, and we can't allow that to happen.

Again, although I've given you mock answers to get you started on becoming fearless and having the confidence to think out loud about how you feel, don't borrow my suggestions. The blank pages that follow are for your own words. Take one more look at the questions, then write down whatever spontaneously comes to your mind.

Answer and Summary Page Of My Fears

1. Am I ready to enjoy life without a fear in the world?

_____

_____

_____

_____

_____

_____

_____

_____

_____

_____

2. Am I entitled to a happy life?

_____

_____

_____

_____

_____

_____

_____

_____

_____

_____

_____

_____

_____

_____

3. To become truly fearless, what would **I** change in my life?

_____

_____

_____

_____

_____

_____

_____

_____

_____

_____

_____

_____

_____

_____

_____

_____

4. After exploring and becoming mindful of my fears, would I end or begin a new relationship?

_____

_____

_____

_____

_____

_____

_____

_____

_____

_____

_____

_____

_____

_____

5. Have I had enough anxiety for one lifetime?

_____

_____

_____

_____

_____

_____

_____

_____

_____

_____

_____

_____

_____

_____

6. Do I want to pass on my fears to my family or my children?

_____

_____

_____

_____

_____

_____

_____

_____

_____

_____

_____

_____

_____

_____

_____

_____

7. Do I want to live in heaven or hell on earth?

_____

_____

_____

_____

_____

_____

_____

_____

_____

_____

_____

_____

_____

_____

_____

_____

Now that you've answered the seven questions and you've explored your most hidden fears, you have taken the first step to enhancing your life. But your job isn't done yet. Just as the song says, "We've only just begun."

I congratulate you for all the groundwork and mindfulness you've put into preparing for your first key—the key of fearlessness, which unlocks the first door to the life you've always longed for.

Fearlessness

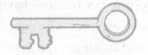

KEY ONE

My dear friend, before you try to awaken your instincts and enhance every aspect of your life, I wholeheartedly recommend that you first search inside yourself. Search deep inside your subconscious mind, which is what my daughter helped me to do when I was lost.

Even though Jacqueline was just a young child, she possessed an empathy and intuition way beyond her years. Sure, Jackie has her own gifts, so I was helped by an especially gifted child. But a child doesn't have to be a psychic (or the daughter of one) to be of help. Despite many beliefs to the contrary, children can help others grow spiritually. There is no age requirement for a person to teach us something valuable. The main requirement is that the person needs to LOVE YOU! And, my daughter loved me. She was then and is now one of my dearest and closest soul mates.

Jacqueline, through her love and fearlessness, helped awaken and enhance my instincts. She pushed and dared me to get well, to find a way back. Despite her reality—having a parent who was very ill—she was a brave explorer who was willing to delve into a place many adults would never go: the subconscious mind.

We need to explore our subconscious because that's where many of our fears began and where they have lived safely tucked away. I know the task of searching into your deep-subconscious may seem difficult, and it may be something you're not too thrilled to unravel. So let's make this easier.

It's Time to Explore

Let's change the term "searching" your deep-subconscious to "exploring" your deep-subconscious. Why the word change? Because it can redirect your consciousness to another place. First of all, the word "exploring" sounds a lot less difficult than "searching." Secondly, it feels less like a chore. Therefore, your consciousness will be excited to have some fun exploring. (And anyway, don't we already have enough chores in our everyday life? I believe many of us have comatose instincts—instincts we haven't yet used—because we're inundated with such busy lives. So the fewer chores, the better, and the more enticing exploring becomes.)

In addition, we usually only search for things we believe to be lost. But our deep-subconscious thoughts or fears aren't lost. They are hidden—or buried deep within us.

Don't be dismayed by their concealment though. We can and we will have a great adventure discovering them, just like taking a voyage to explore uncharted lands for buried treasure. Like that treasure, our fears are buried in an unexplored part of our being, and the fun and the reward is finding them and overcoming them. Once we have overcome them, we take the wheel of our life and we regain control. So becoming aware of your fears will not be a chore or a hardship for you. Instead it promises to be an exciting journey that will bring you treasures beyond your wildest dreams. (You won't have to fear getting lost at sea while you're looking for them, and there sure won't be any pirates for you to worry about as you make your discoveries.)

There's so much to look forward to. Once you master how to navigate your mind you will never have to shoulder the burden of your earlier fears. You'll be overjoyed with what you have accomplished, and you'll look forward to every turn your life makes, even the lopsided ones. You know why? Because there aren't any mistakes, but only more lessons. And the more lessons, the more joyful your life will become—all because you'll be fearless!

If you still aren't convinced that this fearlessness lesson isn't going to be as simple as I'm making it sound, and you don't know if you'll have the time or the patience, or even the guts to follow through, do yourself a big favor. Relax, and enjoy the experience.

Think about this: There are no accidents in life and the fact that you're reading this book is no mere coincidence. If it's not a coincidence, then it's intended for you. Which means you shouldn't find exploring your deep-subconscious to be a tedious task but a joyful, painless enlightenment. It's an easy way to find what you've been subconsciously as well as consciously searching for since the time you could first reason—an easy way to satisfy our desperate need for happiness.

We've been searching for a pain-free, secure, and happy life ever since we were expelled from the safety of our mother's womb. Consider this: Every human being has cried out from the moment they were born. Why? Because of the unknown. Because we were searching for someone to cuddle us and make us feel secure once more. As we grew older, we looked—and most of us are still looking—for someone or something to make us happy and enhance our lives. It seems that it doesn't matter how old we become—we're always on the lookout for happiness. But the easiest lesson you'll learn in this book is that our happiness isn't found with someone or something else—it's found inside us.

There Are No Coincidences

Coincidences happen for a reason, whether you believe it or not. We've been trying to manifest these happenings (coincidences, subconsciously) from our first breath, with the hope that each and every coincidence will bring us closer to our goal for joy.

Most times, what we believe to be a mere coincidence is not a coincidence at all. For example, imagine bumping into an old friend who you were just moments before thinking about. Or bending down to pick up a book that has fallen off a bookstore shelf as you were passing by. You pick it up and look it over with every intention of putting it back in its place on the shelf. But suddenly you discover that you can't bear to part with it and you instinctively feel you must buy the book and take it home with you. That, my friend, was not an accident or a coincidence. It was a tug from the universe to point you in the right direction.

On the road to finding the fulfillment you seek, as we explore, think about the scenarios I just described. A book falling off a shelf as you happen to pass by, or an encounter with an old friend you were just thinking of. Could it be a simple coincidence? Be your own judge.

I believe with every inch and molecule of my being that there is no such thing as coincidence. I believe that the magic the Universe holds comes from the energy emanating from us. This energy can come from our thoughts or our actions. I believe our thoughts and actions create our magic, be it good magic or bad. Think of our good energy or magic as our positive thoughts, and the bad magic as our negative thoughts.

But the magic that the universe and we contain holds no trickery like a witch in a fairy tale. It's nothing like the slick moves of a quick-handed magician who makes things disappear and reappear through sleight of hand. No, our magic is inside all of us.

Our magic is in the answers that are tucked away for us to discover once we leave our fears behind. It can be obtained only once you have the keys that open the door to your rational awakened intuitive self—the self deep inside you that recognizes that there is no such thing as a coincidence. The self that believes a coincidence is a miracle in the making of your best destiny.

The universe uses these invisible intuitive forces, or energies, which most people have learned to define as mere coincidence, to help us overcome the logical way we were raised to think. It's a way of thinking that most are locked in to.

Ah, and at this very moment, I'm receiving one of those invisible celestial nudges (OK, they're not so invisible to me anymore, now that I've become so accustomed to reading the signs over the years), telling me to get you started with discovering the U in you. What's the U in you? Well, the U is a shorthand symbol that represents the undertow in all of us—the part of us that unconsciously holds us back or keeps us down.

Think of the word "undertow." You probably see the ocean, a beautiful sandy beach, with waves crashing at the shore. But just a short way out into the water, there's an invisible force at work—the undertow. The ocean's dreaded undertow captures swimmers unexpectedly and forces them under the surface, preventing them from breathing freely. You see, fear is an undertow that holds us back as well as holds us under. The undertow that comes with our fears pulls us away from finding complete and utter fulfillment in life.

Understanding Your Fears

I'm certain that you are a lot like I used to be when I was fearful. Indeed, my list of fears made Santa's "naughty and nice" Christmas list pale in comparison. You name it, I was afraid of it. I was fearful of the day ahead of me, fearful of what tomorrow would hold, and most of all, fearful of all the things unknown. I was especially fearful when it came to my medical well-being and what would happen to my little girl if I was no longer capable of taking care of her by myself.

There was one thing I was sure of. I knew I needed help to find a way of confronting my fears. I also knew that before I could confront my fears, I had to be mentally and spiritually ready to meet them head on. And when we get to that point, *voila!* We've found the opening that reaches the closed doorways of our fears. I needed big-time help opening my door.

I felt as though I was falling into a deep despair. Not depression—there is a difference. In my case, I despaired that I wouldn't find a way to get better, and I felt as though time was running out. If I didn't find a way to get better soon, my door to the healthy future I had dreamed of would be forever closed.

Depression, to me, means that no matter what good you have in your life, you can't see it because you're in a state of hopelessness. When you're depressed, there are no little moments of joy or satisfaction. In my situation, though there were plenty of times I cried my eyes out, I never reached that state of hopelessness. In fact, the opposite was often true. When I felt even the slightest bit healthier, no matter how small the victory, I was ready to throw a party to rejoice the day. I believe those moments of joy and holding onto those little glimpses of what could last forever gave me courage and kept me from falling into a true depression.

And so I prayed, meditated, and asked the universe and the Divine Holy Spirit to aid me. I asked for help for seven years. But don't worry, I promise you it won't take you seven years to find the keys to your happiness and your life's enhancement. Jackie and I have already done the research for you, and you're going to benefit from our knowledge. We documented all the lessons, objectives, mental exercises, and guide points that we learned throughout our journey, and now we are passing them on to you. We also pass to you our confidence that you'll find your keys to those mindful treasures that the universe is keeping in a safe place for you. I know you'll be retrieving your keys in no time at all.

But the answers won't arrive in a puff of smoke when you snap your fingers. It will take determination, visualization, and a promise to yourself and to all those you hold dear. No matter how tempted you may be to put this book down and save the lessons within its pages to read or study for another day, you must pledge to carry on. Don't wait another day! Do it now! I'll tell you why.

Because tomorrow, the tomorrow you say that you've been hoping for and praying for and waiting not so patiently for, will never come if you procrastinate. Let me ask you one very simple and direct question: Aren't you tired of waiting to enhance and enjoy your life? I'm sure you are, especially if you've picked up this book in your search for answers. The question itself was rhetorical.

So, because we're in total agreement that any kind of procrastination is a bad thing, let's make a promise to each other right here and now that we won't give up on each other. Not now, not ever.

So who am I to ask you to make such a promise? Even though

we may not have met formally and I may not be a family member or your best friend, our lives are forever connected through the collective unconscious of humanity.

Just reading this page that I have written has connected us forever. Because even if you forget the exact words on this page, your subconscious won't forget the lesson it has learned. Most times, I believe that we don't give our intellect the credit it deserves. As an intuitive explorer of consciousness, I can see and feel the energy that surrounds not only my life but also my family. I can also see and feel what people aren't seeing for themselves. I want you to share in my joy of exploration by utilizing the natural gift of your collective unconscious to feel and see the universe as I do, and as so many others have—those who have stopped procrastinating and have finally allowed themselves to live in the moment. When you finally allow yourself to live consciously in the moment, you will be able to see the world as clearly as I do.

Jacqueline and I will stay connected with you and help you learn, as we have done, how to find an opening to the closed doorways to your fears. You can benefit from our experiences.

You see, I took baby steps toward the keys that opened the doors to my awakened instincts. Or, I should say, our awakened instincts—Jacqueline's and mine. I now understand that my daughter's instincts matured and blossomed in record time while mine were reawakening. (It seems the universe was kind to us and allowed one of us to be awake while the other slept). The main reason I've written this book—with the help of my daughter—is to teach you what we had to learn and experience firsthand the hard way, so maybe you won't have to.

I realize I need to drive home this declaration to you, so you don't forget or lose hope along your journey. You must remember that before my daughter and I were ready and able to receive our keys, or the information we needed to make our frightening past just that—a thing of the past—we had to, above all things, have blind faith in ourselves and the universe. We never, ever gave up, and we always anticipated a happy ending. In doing so, we've created a present and future life that we wouldn't exchange for any other.

But let's not forget that I was the one who was blinded in life. I realized that I was the one who had to remove my fears first. Then, I could help my daughter to continue her quest in learning how to become strong not just for me, but for herself and her future. And once I understood my fears and where they came from, my next step was to learn how to let them go and get rid of them forever.

Dancing Around Anxiety

There were times when I attempted to shake off a certain fear or anxiety, and I found it wasn't leaving me as fast as I had initially desired. I'd dance around it (consciously) until I found a way to make it disappear for good. Yes, permanently.

Let me explain. The first thing I had to do was to consciously admit that my anxiety still existed. It didn't own me anymore, but I had to truthfully acknowledge to myself that it was still hanging around. This time, I had an advantage. I knew the fear was there and it was hiding. I just didn't have all the keys to unlock my fear from my psyche.

You see, being aware of our fears, even though we may not have overcome them all, is still empowering. You can live off that power until you master your keys. And I recommend you do it by using this first step, which I call "dancing around your anxieties," until you've overcome them. That goes for whatever anxieties or fears you haven't quite gotten over yet. But be careful not to dance too long. That's not a good thing and can in fact keep you in limbo longer than it should. So keep aware of how long you're dancing around your anxieties after you've determined what they are. Give yourself a week, or two weeks, or maybe two months, but no longer than that. Give yourself a specific timetable to work with. And come on, don't you agree? Don't you think your weary feet would get tired of dancing if you were actually asked to stay on the dance floor for an undetermined amount of time?

Your next step after dancing around an anxiety is to squirrel that anxiety away. Again this is done consciously. Think of squirreling your fears as the same process as storing your winter clothes in the springtime.

You pack your winter clothes in a box and stash it at the bottom of your closet or in your basement because you have no room for them in your drawers along with the current season's attire. So you squirrel them away until the seasons change again. Then, you'll get a chance to go through the box and see what you'll cast aside and what to keep for the following year.

There's one huge difference between storing our clothes in a box and squirreling away our fears at the bottom of our mind. We don't want to hold on to our fears, or salvage any of them for the next season or the year after that. We want them gone for good. I only recommend squirreling a conscious fear while we're working on getting rid of it permanently. This will mean you won't be held down or held back by the fear while we're waiting to dispose of it for good. The whole time you're squirreling you must be aware of what you are doing and that it's only another step you're taking to rid yourself permanently of the fear or anxiety.

When I faced my fears and set them aside, suddenly everything seemed to fall into place perfectly. I could intuitively hear key-like wind chimes dangling in the breeze of my mind, swaying back and forth in the wind, making a joyful and peaceful sound that sang out the melody of hope for our future.

Take the Step. Go on, Jump!

You've probably heard the phrase, "The first step is the hardest." Well, my first step toward finding the first key was exactly the opposite. When I reached Key 1—"F" —fearlessness, it was unseen to the naked eye, but I could feel it in the heart of my consciousness. Key 1 was my brightest key. It was a light in my life that illuminated my hope for my future as well as the future of my daughter. If I hadn't found it, heaven only knows where we'd be today.

And now the universe has given me another nudge to pass on to you what we have learned: the keys and the steps to reach complete mental, physical, financial, emotional, and spiritual happiness.

If you are still unconvinced, or if you're uncertain that you're ready for some deep soul searching, even if your head is beginning to pound with the thought of scanning your consciousness for its deepest fears—I've come up with a few shortcuts to help you get started with the hope that you'll be able to relax your mind in anticipation of the journey ahead.

The first thing I'd like you to do is to leave your anxieties at the doorway of your past and mentally float into your peaceful future. Yes, you read that correctly, float. If you have a fear of water or you're not a strong swimmer, don't be afraid. The universe will not allow you to drown. Make a conscious choice to surrender your anxieties this very minute. If you cannot, than stop reading and take a moment to calm down your inner core and your center.

Okay, you've had enough time to relax. Let's now get started on floating. Please don't think that I'm trying to control your mind or change your way of thinking. No one person can do that. Why not? Because you are in charge of your destiny. Only you can decide when you've had enough failure, depression, anxiety, and remorse.

When you're finally ready to be truly happy, the keys of life will be waiting for you at the doorway of your future—the future you've always dreamed of. I promise you won't have to look very far for the keys because once you relax your fears, the keys will be yours.

As I've been saying, before we go searching for the keys, we first have to get rid of your biggest fears. One of those fears, no doubt, is the fear of delving into your own subconscious. Let's begin by taking some simple mindful steps. Think of these steps as stretching exercises for your psyche. So, just as you would stretch your body before going out for a good run or other physical workout, use these steps to help you stretch your mind and limber up your consciousness. But before our actual exercise begins, we're going to get to know and understand ourselves a little better.

With Fearlessness Comes Respect

An extra component that you will receive when you enhance each phase of your life and master yet another key is the added respect that you'll feel for yourself. In addition to this new self-respect, you'll also acquire a much-deserved wisdom of self and a sense of pride. With those new attainments will come a healthy golden glowing aura that will forever surround your being and define your personal excellence. The universe will acknowledge that aura through signs of synchronicity that only come when your life and soul are centered. And all these gifts will be yours, all thanks to your passionate and diligent work on yourself.

The glow you'll be emitting will not just be sensed by you emotionally, but physically and outwardly for all to see. With your new radiance will come a physical change and a presence of brilliance that all will revere. Don't forget for one minute that you did this all by simply acquiring and mastering each new key. With each key you obtain you'll come closer to achieving a better quality of life. As each key becomes part of your life's key-chain, you will not only develop your mind, but also increase your spiritual growth and strengthen your physical identity. Those parts of you will be enhanced every time you get to know a little more about who you are and where you are headed.

But the big question is: how do you gain the respect you want and deserve? As I mentioned, you will gain the respect you're lacking by mastering each key. But you don't have to wait until you master all seven keys. You can start right now before you read any further. Here's why respect, now, before we continue to learn about the keys of enhancement, is so important. Because without knowing what it means to be respected and why you need to be fearless, why bother?

I don't think you're reading this book to be lied to. I believe you're reading this book to learn and to know what I've learned in life and how I truly feel. I'm no saint. I'm a mere mortal, just like you, and I've learned from all my mistakes. Along the way, the one thing I never lost in my life was the respect and the integrity I have for myself. (I may have unconsciously suppressed it for a while when I was in bad relationships—we all do it one time or another.) Without respect and integrity for yourself, what good is enhancing your job, your beauty, your health—your anything? The fact is our instincts cannot be enhanced or made better without taking back or regaining self-respect. Without it and everything else we learn, this life's journey is worthless.

Here are a few examples of how you may sometimes subconsciously lose respect for yourself. In turn, the person you seek respect from ends up respecting you less. That's because you want and crave respect so much that it becomes a chore rather than a natural response.

The reason for the turn of events is that the person we're trying to gain respect from sees right through our insecurities. Those insecurities become a vampire, sucking up what little respect we did have for ourselves.

Sometimes when we get caught up in a relationship, our own integrity begins to change. We find ourselves agreeing to things we swore our whole life that we would never agree to. We begin to change the course of the life we planned in our hearts from the time we were children. For someone else, we start letting go of our dreams, one at a time. But relationships built on that kind of accommodation never work out. They may seem to, at times, but it's a false success because the person who gave up on his or her dreams is just an empty shell. His or her life was simply filled up with someone else's dreams.

When I speak about changing or agreeing to things we said that we would never change, I don't mean something as simple as changing a dinner reservation. No, we're talking about the big picture of life here.

Here's a perfect example of a woman who was losing herself for the sake of holding on to the wrong person. In the interim, she was unconsciously losing a little more of her self-respect and self-identity every day. The woman had called my radio show, and as it's a call-in show, I was expecting to receive questions.

And so, the woman—let's call her Jodi—called and asked me

some very simple questions about the relationship she was in. But the longer she spoke, the more I was mentally zoning in on her consciousness. I was intuitively made aware that she already knew the answers to the BIG questions. Maybe not to every question, but I knew she was very aware of the most important questions that she was obsessing about every day.

The one question I was certain she already knew the answer to was about her boyfriend. She knew, and I knew, that he never wanted to get married. Even knowing that in her heart of hearts, she was calling me with the hope that I would give her a different answer than the one she had already found with her own instincts. Those instincts had given her the answer a long time ago, and it had reached both her subconscious and her conscious state of mind.

Jodi admitted that she was absolutely aware that her boyfriend didn't want to get married. He had told her his views on marriage when they first started dating. Yet Jodi was holding on to hope that he'd change his mind. So, we cannot put blame on the boyfriend here because he was straight with her from the get-go.

With that said, I still believe he was playing with her mind a little bit suggesting that he may change his mind some day. He was taking her for a little ride, telling her that maybe in a year or two or three they'd get engaged and then maybe get married.

As our conversation continued, I learned that he had already changed the date of their engagement two times. During the course of their live-in relationship they had bought a house together, but it was legally only in his name. On top of that, they also had a baby together.

Now, I'm the last one to pass judgment and say that people must be married in order to have a baby or, in fact, live a wonderful life together forever. But in order for any relationship to have a real chance to last, both parties must be clear and straight from round one—without any of the double-talking this man was giving to Jodi. The couple involved must agree on their life together, from the beginning of the relationship. Jodi was only kidding herself when she told him she was okay with what he wanted, because she never agreed in her heart. She only stayed with him, despite his initial statement that he didn't want marriage, because she kept the hope that one day down the line he'd change his mind.

When Jodi called me that day, she subconsciously wanted me to validate her wish that he would change his mind. Although she denied it at first, she later admitted to herself, as well as to me, that she has always wanted to get married more than anything else in her life. She was praying that he would come around to her point of view.

Think for a moment about how you would have responded to Jodi's questions. Use a pad and pencil, or you can make a mental note of what you would have said to her. It's a valuable and straightforward exercise. Every time we help someone with a problem, we're helping ourselves awaken and brush up on our instincts. Think seriously about it. What would you say to her?

Here's what I told her:

I informed Jodi that she was more at fault here than he was. Instead of blaming him because she wanted marriage and he didn't, she should be straight up with him and tell him how she felt—that she loved him and really wanted marriage to be part of her life. I told her she shouldn't allow her insecurities to hold her back any longer from speaking the truth to him. If marriage was a life dream—if it was something in her heart's treasure chest—she shouldn't compromise her life or her journey for anyone. I told her not to give him an ultimatum, but just to tell him the truth about how she feels. If he responded by saying, "Okay, we'll get married someday," she should tell him that "someday" would not be good enough.

Why wasn't it good enough? Because she was allowing him to dictate her life to fit his life plan and that won't work. You see, if both people in a relationship don't come to a mutual agreement about how or where the relationship is heading, it bodes trouble. Sooner or later, one of them is going to wind up leaving the relationship anyway. They're going to get tired of hearing the question, "When are we going to get married?"

If you hear marriage questions coming out of your own mouth you're making a huge mistake.

I told Jodi to take back her integrity and her self-respect, and tell her boyfriend that he's been pulling her chain, so to speak, for too long. If he loves her the way he said he did from the beginning, then he'll set a date. But she shouldn't give him an ultimatum. He's got to feel that they are both on the same page in life.

Life is too short to wait for someone, or to wait for someone to change. It very well may never happen. So before you fall too deeply for anyone, make sure that from the beginning of your relationship you're not only on the same page, but that you're reading from the same book.

Do not add to your fears by giving yourself away to someone who doesn't have the same life dreams as you do. It's better to walk alone on your own path than walk behind someone who's following his or her own trail. (You'll find more help in self-diagnosing your own lack of respect or insecurities in the "Symptoms of Energy" chapter.)

Expect the Unexpected/ Expect Miracles

KEY 2

As you enter this fourth chapter and come closer to obtaining the second key, "E," make a conscious choice to comprehend the lessons contained here. Why? Because your future happiness may depend on it! Or, the future happiness of someone you love dearly may depend on how awake your consciousness is.

To explain to you beyond a shadow of a doubt how wondrous learning and owning Key 2 is, Jacqueline and I decided to share with you the tale of the miracle of finding Brandy.

Brandy, at the time of this story, was a twelve-week-old golden lab puppy that Jacqueline had purchased, along with a Siberian husky, when she moved into an apartment she shared with a friend after high school. Despite my concerns, Jacqueline is a lot like me, and once she gets an idea in her head, she normally goes with her instincts and does what she sets out to do. And her instincts told her she needed to experience living on her own for awhile.

One cold fall afternoon at around 4:30 p.m., Jackie telephoned me the way she usually did. At first, I thought the call was just to say hello, but as I zoned in on my daughter's energy telepathically, I realized something was wrong, not with her, but with her dog Brandy—Brandy had gotten loose and ran away. Jackie didn't have to tell me with words; I could feel that the dog was lost.

At that point I asked her, "Jackie, where's Brandy? Is she missing?" After finally hearing me echo her thoughts out loud, Jackie, no longer able to hold in her despair, let out a sob and said, "Yes, Mom, Brandy is lost. She got out of the backyard where she was tied up and she ran away, and now it's dark outside and we can't find her!"

I instinctively knew Jackie and I could find Brandy together, so I rushed over. Instinctively I knew Jackie's energy of love for her puppy would be the added ingredient necessary for me to stay in the psychic-eye dog-tracing detective mode. When I arrived, Jackie's friends and neighbors who had gathered in front of her appartment were ready to give up their search because it was getting dark. Annoyed by their laziness and lack of belief in intuition, I grabbed my daughter by the arm and said, "Let's get going and bring Brandy home."

Jackie and I started our search by walking from door to door. When that didn't work we got in my car so we could drive around and see whether we could smell her out. We drove around for an eight to ten block radius shouting at the tops of our lungs, "Brandy girl, where are you?" It was getting darker and colder. Jackie's energy was exhausted and she was about to give up. But I felt Brandy near. I had to keep Jackie's energy from being depleted, so I told her to call on her angels and ask them for help. Armed with the vision of her angel's presence, Jackie found renewed strength and courage and continued to call for Brandy out the car window. Suddenly I had the feeling we had gone too far, and I made a U-turn and went up a small, dark street near a grade school. I looked at Jackie and said, "Brandy was here. I can feel her."

Jackie sat quietly for a moment with her eyes closed and tried to feel her dog. She half-smiled, afraid that she could be wrong, and said, "I think I feel her here too, Mom." As we continued calling, a young boy, about seven years old, came outside of his home to see who was yelling. When I asked if he had seen a small dog, he said, yes, his neighbors had her!

Jackie immediately ran to the house. As we waited for the neighbor to open up her door, I prayed with every ounce of my soul and asked all my angels to please let it be Brandy. Finally, the woman answered the door with my daughter's Brandy in her arms.

We found Brandy because we didn't give up and we used Key 2, "E," Expect the Unexpected/Expect Miracles. We received just what we expected. But there's a synchronicity to this story that is even more miraculous than finding Jackie's dog. While Jackie hugged Brandy, I looked at the little boy who was now standing with his mother and I said to him, "Do you know what you are?" And he said, "No, what am I?" "You're an earth-angel," I answered. His mother said, " It's funny that you called him an angel because do you know what his name is? My son's name is Angel." Then I cried, and thanked God and the universe and all our angels for their help in finding Brandy.

Music to My Ears

We've all heard the saying, "It's music to my ears." Finding Brandy was music to my ears, and that's what life should be like—music to our ears. And in writing this chapter, and thinking so much about keys, I realized that music was a key to opening and awakening our consciousness.

A musical key is defined as a series of tones bearing a specified relationship to one another. The word "key," as used in this book, has more than one meaning. The first definition that we've used is "a means to unlock the closed doors to our subconscious."

The second definition is "to strike and find harmony in life," and in doing so, you will see and feel how easily you will learn how to play your life's song, and that's with enjoyment and amusement. When we find the right chords in life, they will resonate within us, awakening every instinct, every thought and aspect of our life, including everything we come in contact with. If everything is harmonious, everything that we come in contact with will be melodious, just like the sound of a perfect chord when it is played on a stringed instrument like a guitar or a piano.

How do we bring our higher consciousness and awareness to our life? Easy—by striking the chords that will resonate and awaken our instincts.

When I listen to music, I hear, feel, and see it. The vibratory rhythms of the sounds bring me closer to discovering new facts about myself that had gone undiscovered before. So fundamentally, I live my life like a beautiful symphony now that I've unmasked my hidden fears with the help of music harmony. I may not be one of the world's great musical conductors, or a brilliant composer like Beethoven, but I know when my instincts are in tune. When they are, my life achieves clarity, becoming more pleasant, floatingly harmonious, and synchronistic. And when you reach this point, nothing and no one's lies or negative attitudes will get to you. And when our lives flow harmoniously and our instincts are thoroughly alive and kicking, then our consciousness finally reaches its full potential.

Striking the Right Chords,
Secret Recipes and Hope

I know that when some of you first read this chapter's title, Key 2—"E," you may have momentarily forgotten that the title was taken from the acrostic that was mentioned in the beginning of the book. Let me remind you once again. It's FEARNOT, and Key 2 is the is the word's second letter, E.

I consider this chapter to be my secret recipe for enhancing your life and acquiring what you've been hoping for since before you knew the definition of the word "hope."

Think you've always known the meaning of the word hope? There was a time that you didn't. Let's do a little psychological regression. For just a minute, I'd like you to imagine that you can see yourself as a newborn baby in a hospital nursery, crying your little eyes out. If you're having trouble picturing yourself, then picture any newborn baby for now.

The baby is crying. But why? To get some attention from a nurse? Or because crying is good exercise for the lungs?

No, you were crying because you were hoping (before you knew what hope was) that someone would come and pick you up, and comfort you or feed you. And all the while your new family was playing coochie-coo with you through the nursery glass windows, you were crying and hoping intuitively that one of those faces staring down at you would actually do something for you.

So now without further ado, I am now going to share with you my secret recipe to enhancing your life using Key 2—"E."

MARY'S SECRET RECIPE

Ingredients:

> One-third cup of life from the music retrieved from your soul;
> One-third cup of harmony that vibrates positive energy
> throughout your life and,
> Two-thirds cup of love, security, and hope for your future.

Stir gently and mix three quarters of the ingredients generously throughout your body, mind, and soul. It will cook naturally as your instincts become awakened. Pour the rest of the ingredients into the universe. That, my friends, is the recipe for a life without anxieties and fears or trepidations. Prepare it as often as necessary and don't be afraid to share.

Now that I've let my secret recipe out of the bag, let's get back to this chapter's life lesson.

As you read further into this chapter and once Key 2 becomes part of your daily life, you will appreciate the enormous value that's contained in this key. Incorporating "E" into your everyday routine will be as easy as breathing out and in and just as unnoticeable. Like breathing, the only time you'll become aware of it is when you stop doing it—and it's just as important.

Don't be hesitant to add "E" to your life. It's simple as adding three tiny lessons to the natural rhythm of your life (coming in the next section.) In doing so you will strike a chord that in turn will awaken your senses effortlessly and melodiously, as simply as if you were playing a musical chord on a grand piano.

Your Personal Piano Lessons

Speaking of the piano, as part of your first lesson, imagine that you're sitting in front of a beautiful polished Steinway piano. The piano in this case will represent your life.

Next, I'd like you to imagine that this book, especially this chapter, is your music teacher.

I'm sure most of you are aware that in order for someone to learn to play a musical instrument properly, you have to take lessons. Even if you took music lessons as a child and hated them, I promise that the following lessons will bring the music of life back into yours, and you'll enjoy the education. The lessons are as follows:

Lesson One: You must have a passion as well as a yearning for the music to become a part of you.

Lesson Two: You should explore and study your instrument. Know how and why it makes the music that it does. In addition, you must be present while you're studying your lessons—not just physically but soulfully.

Lesson Three: Practice, practice, and then practice some more—that is, if you want to be a great musician and not just someone who dabbles or plays occasionally.

In order for you to realize and understand just how valuable Key 2—"E," is, it's extremely important for you to realize and visualize that your life is an instrument that needs tender loving care and fine tuning. Because just as the instruments we play need to be tuned every now and then, we also need to tune or tweak our minds to make sure all our keys and chords are in harmony with our being.

And, in order for us to achieve all the seemingly unexpected miracles, we must treat ourselves the same way we might expect a rock star or a famous orchestra conductor to be treated.

Think about every great musician, rock group, singer, or even dancer whom you hold in high regard. None of them were born with an automatic ability that made everyone around them respect their talents and think they were extraordinary. Each of them had to practice. Practice with a passion for their craft. This is what they had to do to make their talents seem easy. For us to make it to the Carnegie Hall stage of life, we must have that passion and belief that the unexpected—wondrous things—can happen in our lives. Is your future happiness and enlightenment worth the practice and dedication it may require for you to create the best you that you can be? You bet you're worth it! We're all worth it!

Please don't shun the idea of practicing to make yourself better, because when we practice, we receive praise, and not just from strangers or an audience. When we feel good about our own accomplishments, we are able to praise ourselves without arrogance or ego for a job well done.

Expecting the Good

When we feel happy about the work we've accomplished and our once-darkened instincts are drenched with the bright light of awareness, we can expect miracles to follow right behind. I'm talking about the miracles and unexpected gifts that the universe has been holding for us like a Christmas present hidden behind a locked door. The presents have been waiting there until we found our own set of keys to unlock our fears. Then we're able to receive our greatest wishes, hopes, and dreams.

Key 2, signified by the letter "E," is the *Essence* of our thoughts and *Enlightenment,* which in turn will enable us to not be cynical while we're waiting to "Expect the unexpected." When you hear "Expect the unexpected," never allow yourself to think of that phrase in a negative sense. Believe it or not, some people were brought up to believe that the expression is another way of saying, "You never know when the other shoe will fall!"

But fortunately, the negative connotation couldn't be further from the truth. Key 2—"E," actually means that we should expect the miracles we've been hoping for even though the odds don't seem to be in our favor, even though the probability of receiving our wishes is low, even if things look mighty dim and every logical bone in our bodies is saying, "No way, this is never going to happen, the odds are stacked up against me!" Ignore those negative thoughts once and for all, and keep on expecting the unexpected.

There are times some people reply negatively to a positive reading I've just given them, and I'm truly disappointed. It might be a reading where I've stretched and projected my intuition to its highest vibratory level, searching and exploring not only their consciousness, but the consciousness of any and all those intertwined in their lives. I believe a big part of my job is to help people get rid of the idea that someone or something is holding them back from their dreams or their best destiny. For example, I gave one woman a reading, telling her how she had to change to become the woman she wanted to be. I told her to get rid of the boyfriend who was abusing her mentally and physically. She could have replied with many things, but all she could ask was, "Are you sure we won't make it together?"

On those occasions, I wonder, "When will they be finally ready to let go of the small stuff?" Granted, some people have huge issues to deal with. But no matter what size a person's problem, we can get around it by using our instincts. When I have a problem and I'm done being worried about it, I put it in its correct place. That's in the garbage, along with the other dilemmas, issues, or problems that serve no purpose other than making us anxious and fearful.

When I do get a client or friend who has those pessimistic thoughts, I ask them that exact question, "When will you finally be ready to let go of the small stuff?" I don't expect them to answer me. I don't need to because I can read their consciousness, especially if I've been zoning in on them during our session. It's even easier for me to sense, after spending time exploring someone's consciousness, whether they have changed from their pessimistic outlook to an optimistic one.

The Virtual Neurosurgeon

How can we teach the people in our lives who have come to expect slim pickings from life to expect the unexpected miracles that are waiting for them? It's quite simple. All we have to do is to teach them to be a virtual neurosurgeon who can operate on themselves. That is, without any sharp instruments.

Why a virtual neurosurgeon? Because neurosurgeons are trained to fix and understand how our brains react inside and out. Imagine yourself as your own Dr. McDreamy and visualize that you're removing from your thoughts all the junk that's been keeping your brain from seeing and sensing things clearly. In essence, I want you to learn how to rewire your brain and the neurons that control the way you interpret your thoughts. You know the ones I'm talking about: the ones that say anything unexpected can't be good.

But "E" means exactly the opposite, thank goodness. It means, "Expect the unexpected. Expect miracles that cannot be rationalized."

So for those of you who were brought up to believe that life is about waiting for the other shoe to drop, stop thinking that way immediately! The other shoe isn't going to fall unless you believe it will. Then you will cause it to fall.

From now on, when your life seems to be getting out of hand and you seem to be having trouble believing that your expected miracles will happen, open up this book and peruse the chapters. Get a refresher course on awakening your instincts. It may also be a good idea to keep a copy on hand in your bag, briefcase, or backpack. This way you never have to feel like you're alone in a difficult situation.

I recommend that you think of Key 2 with regard to all your dreams and aspirations. Never forget that the letter "E" means to expect the miracles that you've been praying, hoping, and wishing would happen, no matter how tiny a chance. The next time you feel downhearted about anything that's going on in your life, think to yourself: "I'm expecting the unexpected," and "I will believe in miracles." Why? Little miracles actually occur to each and every one of us every day, but most of us are unaware of them because we expect our miracles to be huge, billboard-type special events. Events like the parting of the Red Sea or winning the lottery. Can miracles like that ever happen? Absolutely, but they're much rarer than the smaller ones we receive every day.

The knowledge of "E," our second key, will bring you closer to unlocking yet another door, once thought impenetrable, that most of us have subconsciously kept closed even when we're in the process of asking the universe for yet another wish. I know that I'm not the only one who believes that miracles actually exist. If you believe you have obtained all the knowledge you need with regard to getting what you want from life, you're wrong. There is always more to learn. If the door to your subconscious is jammed, all you need is a little help opening the door.

That's where the virtual neurosurgeon comes in. You can control your thoughts and your attitudes, and use your senses to see things more clearly. You have the power to rewire those neurons.

A Locksmith, and Six Steps to Help You Attain Key 2—E

For those of you whose instinctive doors have gotten stuck when life's complications come around—and yes, there's always something knocking at our door—don't back away or back down. You can handle anything life throws your way. I'd like you to allow me to be your locksmith—one who comes prepared with the keys you've been waiting for. A locksmith can get you closer to your goal, and with the right passion, study, and practice, you can learn to be your own locksmith. You can hone in and take the keys for yourself, and you can learn how to use them to unlock your own doors.

Here are six additional small steps to memorize into your consciousness. They will help you attain the key "E," which will unlock the doors to your awaiting miracles.

Step One: SEE YOURSELF WORTHY OF A MIRACLE

If you're single and the one miracle you want more than any other is to find your soul mate, you will. But you'll find Mr. or Ms. Right only if you believe you're worth it and that you're equal in every way to the person you're manifesting in your mind's eye. Remember, no one is better and more worthy of your love than you are.

For those of you who are dating or wish to be dating in the near future, never accept crumbs from the new person you meet. Expect the whole cake. What do I mean by that? If you're hoping for a boyfriend or girlfriend, don't keep dating someone who tells you right out that they don't want a serious relationship. You're not going to change their mind. If they've been honest with you and they've told you they don't want a commitment, you'll be accepting crumbs if you keep the relationship going. You're worth the whole cake.

For those of you who are already married, engaged, or have a steady commitment, ask yourself as well as your loved one some very simple questions with regard to your relationship. This is something you should do every six months. Six months isn't so frequent that you'll sound as though you're nagging or insecure, and it's a short enough time span to keep your instincts sharpened and your telepathy clear with each other. Call it your A.I. Pow-Wow (Awakened Instincts Pow-Wow) and ask these questions:

"Are we happy with the way our relationship is going?"

Don't just ask yourself this question, ask your partner, too. In doing so, you'll clear up any slight misunderstandings you may have had within the past six months. Perhaps something happened that you never discussed as deeply as you wanted to at the time, maybe because you got distracted and forgot, or maybe you buried your problems within your subconscious.

It's extremely important that you accent the positive aspects of your relationship at this time, too. Sure, this is a time to bring up concerns you may have, and to talk about conditions that made you feel uncertain or insecure within the past six months. But don't just pick on the bad or shaky moments (and remember not to sweat the small stuff!)

"How can we make our relationship better than it has been?"

This question should not carry a negative undertone, but should reflect respect for one another. If you feel that your job is done, or that your A.I. Pow-Wow is over because you and your partner have already given a positive response to the first question, remember there's always room for improvement and growth in any relationship. Good relationships sometimes fall by the wayside because we believe everything is perfect and no one is complaining. But there are always areas that can be improved, and your happiness can grow, if you're willing to ask how you can do it.

The following are intuitive awareness reminders that I recommend you keep in your consciousness—right there in the forefront of your instincts.

1. You don't always have to wait six months for your A.I Pow-Wow. You can have your heart-to-heart every three months if you feel the need to, but unless some major issues arise, do not have these Pow-Wows too often. Of course, keep your instincts awakened and use your better judgment in your daily life, but don't be one of those needy people who are always asking their loved ones, "Do you love me?" You'll just be banging your loved one over the head with too many questions. And if you do, you'll be looking for someone like me to help direct you and your relationship back on course.

2. Don't forget to look for the good in each other, daily. You should make a list of all the good things your loved one has done for you, or has done for him- or herself, that you've noticed since your last A.I. sit-down. You don't have to wait three or six months to give your partner a compliment or to express your appreciation. That's something you should do every day or every night before you go to bed. But when you are complimenting your sweetheart, make sure that it's sincere and that you're not just coming up with something nice to say just for the sake of being kind. Although we can never be too kind, we can come across as too needy or insecure, and that's not a good thing! Remember this book is

about awakening instincts, and let's hope the instincts that will be awakened won't just be yours, but your loved one's also. Your partner will be aware if you're stretching to find a compliment. At those times, you'll wind up making the person you're directing the kindness toward feel as though you think he or she is in desperate need of your praise. That will cause some discomfort, and you may actually make a good thing turn bad.

3. Can you do anything right? Be nice, but don't be too nice . . . Ask questions, but not too many . . . I know, it sounds as though no matter what you say, you risk saying the wrong thing. If you've gotten that feeling then, *voila!* We're on the right track. If it feels hard now, that's because your instincts are asleep. But once they're awake, then it's as easy as brushing your teeth in the morning. Your instincts toward each other won't be work, but will come very naturally to both of you.

4. Don't forget about your children! They, and you as a parent, can benefit from A.I.s. You can incorporate the same types of questions when you sit down with them. Use an appropriate set of questions for each child's age group. You may want to sit down with your kids much more frequently, per-

haps on a weekly basis. Nothing too in-depth or elaborate, but a child deserves a compliment every day, and because they are children, they will make many more mistakes. Their sit-down times with you will help to keep them on track.

Step Two: MAKE A "LIFE'S EXPECTATION LIST" OF THIRTEEN THINGS

Thirteen items, a baker's dozen. I've thrown in an extra expectation for good measure. You're going to create a list of thirteen miracles you want to happen to you.

Forget the silly notion that miracles and/or extraordinary lives only happen to other people. They will happen to you as long as you expect them without anxiety.

Start your list on a regular sheet of paper or enter your list in your journal. This is your life, and these are your desires, so never feel foolish with what you decide to put on your "Life's Expectation List." Don't worry that these wishes may seem extreme to you. You can ask for the moon if you care to.

I must also point out that your list can increase or decrease as time goes on. Your list should be somewhat in flux. As you receive your expectations or a long-awaited miracle comes to pass, the number of wishes on your list may decrease. When you reach one of the accomplishments you've listed, put a little check or a star next to it on your list. When you're done checking off your gifts, ask yourself what you want to accomplish next. No, don't ask only what you want to acquire next, but what your soul needs to become a better person, not just for yourself but for everyone else in your universe. After meditating on how you'd like to replenish your list back up to your baker's dozen, then with pen in hand, and loving and positive thoughts for your future in mind, enter your new hopes on your list.

Step Three: WORK WITH ENTHUSIASM

Work with enthusiasm on your expected miracles. How? Practice visualizing your goals until it become effortless. Do so with the same intensity you would if you were studying a musical instrument that you were passionate about mastering. Okay, I'm certain that many of you reading this step are thinking that you could never imagine being passionate about studying a musical instrument. If that's the case, then let's try getting into the head or the mind-set of someone we probably all know—someone who does have a passion about a musical instrument. The first person I think of when I think of music and passion is Billy Joel.

Just for the fun of it, think for a moment of what it would be like to be Billy Joel, one of the most famous contemporary pianists and talented singer/songwriters of our day. (Of course, my opinion is most definitely biased because I've adored Billy Joel's work since he cut his first single. But my opinion, as most people who are over thirty years of age would know, is shared by millions of other fans.)

Okay, so now you've got the picture of what it may be like to be not just a rock star, but a passionate musician who takes pride in his work and whose music comes from his soul. When he pounds the keys of his piano, he does so not just with his fingers, but with his heart and soul.

How can I be so sure that when Billy Joel plays he does so with such enthusiasm? Because if he didn't, we wouldn't still be humming and singing and listening to his songs, some of which were written twenty-five years ago.

You see, when you work with enthusiasm, it's catching. It takes hold of you, but it also takes hold of anyone it touches. So today for your homework assignment, listen to Billy Joel's song, "The Piano Man." The song is about a talented young man who works in a bar, singing and playing his piano for the bar's customers. He sings about his wishes of one day making it big in the music industry, and a patron of the bar says, "Man, what are you doing here?" The comment was a compliment to the genius and the enthusiasm of the Piano Man's work.

So whether you're a hopeful rock star, movie star, mom-to-be, or a rocket scientist, work on your career and your dream with enthusiasm so that twenty-five years later you can look back and still be happy with your song, your movie, your choices, and your life.

Step Four: DON'T SHARE YOUR DREAMS

Don't share your dreams or your unexpected gifts with nonbelievers or pessimists. If you share your dreams, hopes, and prayers with someone who doesn't believe in miracles or unexpected gifts, you may begin to doubt yourself or your upcoming achievements.

For example, let's say you've gotten wind that a new position will be opening up very shortly at your place of employment. It's the position you've been dreaming about from the first day you took your current job. You've been secretly praying or hoping that one day the position would open, even though when you've mentioned your hopes to your boss or other co-workers, their replies were always that you shouldn't hold your breath waiting for such a position. But lo and behold, what do you know? Two years down the road, you hear from a friend in Human Resources that the job will most definitely be opening in just a few short months. When you hear this wondrous news your first impulse is tell someone, right? Wrong! But wrong not just because of the negative energy. If you want that job and the universe is allowing you to hear about it before anyone else, take it as a sign that everyone wasn't supposed to know about it. If they were, the job would have been announced to everyone at once. No, the universe is giving you a heads-up to gather yourself, to redo your resume, and to make a list of your special attributes before anyone else has a chance to prepare. I know it sounds unfair, but life as we all know isn't always fair. Some things are meant for some people and not for everyone.

But the most significant reason not to share your dream with regard to the new position is because of the naysayers who said you'd never get the position. (By the way, the position became a reality in the first place most likely because of your dreams manifesting.) Why do we have to keep quiet with negative people or nonbelievers? Because some people just want others to stay stuck in the life they are used to seeing them in, and God forbid someone else should achieve more than they have. Why, if that happened, their egos couldn't deal with it.

So before you get all excited and prematurely share your joy that your life dream may come true, hold on and think. Think about how the person you're about to tell will react. Act out the scenario in your mind before you actually say the words. See yourself saying exactly what you want to say to your co-worker, then close your eyes and "feel" the other person's mental response.

If you believe he will encourage you wholeheartedly, then by all means spill the beans. But if your instincts tell you he may say you're getting in over your head or that you'll never get the job, then keep quiet. His response could put a doubt in your mind that you may find nearly impossible to get out.

Step Five: CLEAN UP THE CLUTTER IN YOUR LIFE—LITERALLY!

One way to help clean up your life and remove unwanted clutter is by learning how to balance the space in your home or office. The area you work and live in should be as balanced as you'd like your life to be.

If you leave your home without making your bed, don't expect your day to be as perfect as it could be. If you leave dirty dishes in your kitchen sink overnight, you'll not only invite insects in your home, but you're setting yourself up for a mess from the beginning of your day!

Step Five, as you can see, is one of the most important steps you'll ever take. This step doesn't take any grandiose expertise. You can begin learning it as soon as you're capable of comprehending and walking.

When I talk to people about reducing clutter (especially when I explain to children how they can expect to receive what they want from life), I hear a lot of moaning and groaning from them with regard to cleaning up their personal space. Honestly, I believe most adults don't like the idea of cleaning either, but nevertheless, it must be done. And it's got to be done by the person wanting to receive life's gifts.

This step can be tackled from any age starting from two to 102.

Two-year-olds may seem a little young to be given this step, but that's not so. Toddlers know how to pick up their toys when they want to play with them, right? So if they can pick up those toys to play, they can pick them up to put them away. It's up to the adults in charge to teach children how to follow the steps of life. If we teach our children from an early age to be responsible for their actions, and if we allow them to use their intelligence to know they must keep their personal space clean and clear, they'll have less trouble enjoying their instincts when they get older.

If you're 102, I'm sure the universe won't mind if you hire a cleaning person to give you a hand. But in most cases, unless a person has a disability and cannot physically clean his or her space, then, everyone must clean up after themselves! Everyone!

Begin, as I said, with your personal space. If you live with a roommate or share a home with someone, be it partner, spouse, or child, I would recommend that the other person or persons sharing the energy and space of your home do the same. If they choose not to help keep the energy uncluttered, I can guarantee that you won't be living with them too much longer. Or, if you continue your living arrangements, they will be far from harmonious.

Step Six: SING!

And last but far from least, here is your sixth step: Sing! Every day, listen to a positive or uplifting song that you can sing along with.

And exactly where should you sing? Anywhere and everywhere. There's a quote I have hanging in my office that reads, "Sing as though no one can hear you!" I believe it's a terrific instruction. When we sing, we should let our guard down and just belt one out!

To let you in on one of my little secrets, I do my best singing in the car or when I'm singing with my dog. Yep, I said it. I sing with my dog. I sing and he howls. He's a beagle named Chance, and he loves the chance to sing whenever he can. If we observe our animals carefully, they have a lot to teach us.

Don't be afraid to belt your song out no matter where you're singing. (I don't expect you to start singing a the top of your lungs at work or anywhere else that's inappropriate.) You need to let the music run through you. When you do, it raises the vibratory levels of your consciousness and thus raises your awareness and your instincts.

But if you're the shy type and you prefer not to sing out loud, even if it's in your own home, then hum along with a happy song on the radio, or sing silently in your mind, or maybe even dance around the room. Whichever way, you'll be moving, and you'll change your energy level from sedate to awake. Any way you decide to get your positive juices flowing in the morning, do it. And remember, as long there's a song in your heart, there will be life and positive energy running through your veins.

Arise to Every Occasion

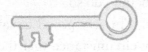

KEY 3

Arise to every occasion. You're probably wondering how arising to an occasion, or stepping up to the plate (which in my book means the same thing), can help awaken and enhance every aspect of your life. Well it can, and Jackie and I would like to explain the concept.

Jackie has seen a lot of what happens when people don't step up and do the right thing in life. These people, whom she calls slackers, are those she considers to be lazy. Some have a sense of entitlement and expect the best grades, the best careers, and the best of everything in life without having to work hard for it. Others procrastinate when they are asked to do something extra for school or for a friend. Jackie says she sees these as sorry, lonely young people.

Jackie says if they don't learn to step up to the plate of life now while they are young, by the time they're ready to start a family or a terrific career, what they want won't be ready for them. They haven't earned the karma and the understanding of why they should be naturally ready, willing, and able to step up when the universe calls upon them to do so.

And as her mother, I'm very proud to say that Jackie always tries to arise to every circumstance that the universe throws at her. We'd like to teach you how to be ready, too.

For the moment, let's begin with the dictionary meaning of the word arise, which is, "to awaken, ascend, or to come into being." You can see by that definition that arising to an occasion is equal to becoming awake to your surroundings and your instincts. And that's why the phrase "arise to every occasion" is this chapter's theme. I want you to wake up your senses, and they will wake up as you arise to life's occasions.

You see, in order for us to completely and totally awaken our instincts to their maximum potential, we must first exercise our senses. It's similar to the way we would exercise if we wanted to get our physical body into great shape, with one notable exception: we won't have to break a sweat doing so.

When we exercise our bodies, we're awakening and teaching our muscles, tendons, joints, ligaments, and our vital organs to work at their highest potential. In doing so, we're making ourselves healthier than we were before. It helps if we also maintain a healthy diet and lifestyle. If you've made up your mind that you truly want to stay in great shape, you know that you can't just exercise every now and then. You need a daily routine and there has to be continuity to your workouts. Now, exercising your instincts and arising to every occasion is a lot easier to do than working out or going to the gym. And I'll let you in on a little secret that you'll be thrilled to know—you won't have to give up a single carbohydrate to find success.

I joke about exercise and eating right, but I have found that a healthy lifestyle in reality makes it much easier for you to reach your true potential. I consider it a real requirement, that is, if you want to heighten your awareness to the max. A healthy body—one without excessive alcohol or overmedication—makes it much easier for you to be awake to what's going on around you.

Wait, you're saying, "I do arise to every occasion already." But I'm telling you that we don't. You certainly don't need a psychic's eye to see that we don't arise to every occasion that the universe puts in our path. Just look at the way some people around you respond to a stressful situation. Or how they react to a situation they simply don't want to be bothered with at the moment, often because they may think it's just too hard to take on. When I sense that there's something I, or someone else around me, may be shirking from, I give a yell. "Too hard? Too bad! Just do it!" That's right, I mentally yell at myself if I'm the one who's having second thoughts about arising to an occasion, or to an intuitive exercise that life is putting in my path. It's all right there for me to learn from.

Rally!

I borrowed the word "rally" from a dear friend who happens to be a physician. For years now, whenever she's tired, she uses the word, "Rally!" or the expression, "Rally to the occasion!" She's done this to encourage herself and to push herself ever since her college and medical school days.

The word did something to me when I heard her use it. Of course, I had heard the word used many times before, but when she said it, I got chills. I knew that if I used it the way she did, and owned it as part of my being and it became one with my consciousness, it would help me. Once I adopted her mantra as my own, I've been rallying to arise to every occasion that comes my way.

In other words, I'm encouraging myself to allow my instincts to be turned up a notch by exercising my instincts with every new task. I ask myself to find the time and find the strength to arise to whatever occasion that the universe has thrown at me and to give it my best shot.

That is, of course, as long as it's something that I can actually physically do without putting myself and my other obligations at risk.

Listen, I didn't write this chapter for the sake of mentally beating up my readers. I want *them* to finally stop beating themselves up after the fact. I know from firsthand experience that we do mentally beat ourselves up when we don't arise to an occasion, whether we're aware of it or not. We're only human, and it's not a crime to try to avoid overextending ourselves, or to say no when someone asks us for a favor. But I believe we're all guilty of doing this too often, because it's human nature to just say, "I'm too tired. I've got to go." Or, "I can't right now. I don't have the time," when certain situations arise. It's sometimes a form of self-defense: in all truth maybe we really don't think we have the time or the strength to take on one more thing, or find the extra hour or two to accomplish an additional task.

But you can beat this feeling. I've found that when the opportunities to exercise our instincts come our way, we should step out of the picture for a moment before we say yes or no. We should take a look at our mental agenda through our third eye—our intuitive eye—which we spoke about earlier.

If you're like most of us, you've probably found yourself ignoring the obvious at times, simply because you don't want to overextend yourself. But don't be too hard on yourself. Arising to every occasion is a work in progress. It's not just a lesson or declaration you can memorize and then be done with. Arising to every occasion has to become part of your life, and it must come to you naturally, without thinking. Then you'll be able to receive the full benefits that being awake to every occasion can bring.

You can achieve the highest level of consciousness possible when you make it your business to stay awake and avoid running from your responsibilities. Never make excuses for why you can't do something you know deep down you probably can. When you awaken your consciousness, you stimulate all your other instincts and senses to come alive and stay animated when the little everyday issues come up in life. You know the ones I'm talking about: the situations that give you a choice to either sit back and do nothing, or arise to the occasion and do something to help or change someone's life. If you look back and analyze different scenarios in your life where you think you might have slacked off, I'm sure you'll find that other things in your life seemed to have gone wrong soon afterward. Or something didn't work out the way you hoped it might. Why? Because the situation you thought you couldn't handle was most likely a synchronicity or a sign or a journey you were meant to either help with or observe in order to keep your own life balanced and centered.

Batter Up!

The other expression I mentioned at the start of this chapter, "stepping up to the plate," has basically the same meaning as "arise to every occasion." But this phrase carries some additional significance that should be mentioned here.

The phrase comes from the game of baseball. A batter—the player holding a baseball bat—steps up to home plate and prepares to hit the ball thrown by the pitcher.

But the batter doesn't just want to hit the ball to get to first base. His goal is usually to hit the ball out of the park, or hit a home run.

Now home runs are hard to come by, but every batter "steps up to the plate," with the hopes of taking their best swing at the ball. That's exactly what we have to do if we are to arise to every occasion. We have to see every circumstance as an opportunity to step up to the plate of life and allow our instincts to take a swing at the ball the universe is pitching at us. When our instincts are exercised that way, we not only enhance our life, but we can enjoy learning just how far our instincts have grown every time we step up to the plate—or with every occasion that arises.

You see, we only have one life and just so many times at bat. Think of every occasion when you didn't take a swing as a life lesson you've shut your eyes to—a chance to enhance your life that you've passed on.

So, when your next time at bat comes, and it may come today, put your best foot forward, get a tight grip on the bat, and take your best swing.

Hold on to the visualization of a baseball player hitting a home run. Keep rewinding the tape in your brain and see it again and again until it becomes second nature to you. If you haven't gotten the picture yet, then keep practicing and you will. Don't miss out on an opportunity to hit one of life's lessons out of the park.

It Doesn't Take a Brain Surgeon

I hope the discussion of those two phrases has made this chapter simple for you to understand. No, not simple because you're not intelligent enough to understand my concepts, but because I am a very simple person. Let's just say I simply call them as I see them (a little like an umpire in a baseball game), with no fancy terminology included to try to make myself seem or feel more important than I really am.

Of course I could use some smarty-pants words to make myself sound oh so smart and brainy. But I won't. Some may say my style of writing is easy reading, and if they do, then I've accomplished what I've set out to do. Write simply the way I see things.

Scientists, I believe, have to refine their methodology and analyze their data because most of them were not born as intuitives. Most were taught to look at things in a logical and factual way. But I've found when scientists test people like me, people who intuitively arise to every occasion and exercise their instincts daily, the PhDs of the world are very surprised to find just how accurate our instincts and intuition are.

Some scientists have called me a lay scientist because I explore my instincts and journal my findings in the same way a scientist would record data on an experiment. I just do what comes naturally to me, and I'm here to tell you that you too can control and journal your instincts without a doctorate and without being born with any exceptional gifts. We are all born with instincts that are ours for the taking, but life sometimes complicates and confuses our natural abilities. When that happens, it sometimes seems difficult to clear away the cobwebs.

Here are a few guide points worth keeping in your mind, or you can write them down as reminders. Just as I borrowed the word "Rally!" Jacqueline and I are passing along our lessons to you.

Guide Points and Key Points to Remember

1. Never do any job or favor halfheartedly.
2. Never put limitations on your dreams.
3. Pledge that you will set new standards for your instincts.
4. If you want more money or a new job or new position, don't put limitations on what you're willing to do, or how hard you're willing to work. (Of course, only do what you're physically and morally capable of, but don't allow a few extra hours a week at a new position to stand in your way to your future.)

5. Be thankful and grateful for every new life project that comes your way and makes you exercise your instincts.

6. Remember that the universe is sending you these gifts, though sometimes they may appear to be burdens. These gifts are a way for you to enhance your life.

7. Don't be afraid to become an independent thinker. If you believe you're an independent thinker already, start using these rules, and you ain't seen nothing yet!

Increase Your Creativity

Creativity is a way to improve yourself on every level. If you think, "No way, I'm not a creative person," this section is especially for you. Every person has the ability to delve into herself with original thoughts and ideas, and creative processes. That doesn't mean you have to pick up a paintbrush and decorate a canvas worthy of an art museum. There are many kinds of creativity, and I'm going to tell you how to recognize yours.

Step One: BRAINSTORMING!

The first step to increasing your creativity is brainstorming.

What's brainstorming? It's an idea-generating technique that lets us break out of our normal way of thinking and to broaden our thinking habits, so we can think out of our safe-box. Brainstorming allows us to consider more than one solution to a problem or an activity.

I'm sure if you work in an environment where you operate sometimes as part of a team, such as public relations firms, law offices, or sales offices, you've experienced brainstorming at your business. The technique of brainstorming can be used by an individual or a group.

Brainstorming innovator Alex Osborn coined the term brainstorming for a session intended to set goals for a situation in which more than one person is involved. Osborn recommends an ideal group size of twelve. I think the best size for a brainstorming group is between two and ten people. Sometimes when too many people are involved in brainstorming in the workplace or at home, conflicting egos can cause arguments to erupt.

The brainstorming method that's worked best for me on the job is to call a meeting of the staff and start asking everyone what their ideas are, without any drama or chaos. People can then volunteer whatever ideas they may have to solve the problem at hand.

Brainstorming is a terrific way to spawn creative thinking. Brainstorming and creative thinking teach us to open up to alternative ideas. Creative thinking enhances our mental and spiritual growth by helping us evolve to a higher thought process and a higher vibratory energy. And so, when the universe sends us a message or situation that will allow us to arise to the occasion, I use creative thinking to meet the challenge.

You're probably wondering if we can brainstorm on our own, with the purpose of enhancing our lives and getting ourselves out of our limbo state of thinking. Of course we can. When it comes to creative thinking, most times we just don't know where to start. That's where brainstorming comes in, and that's what the technique was created for.

Step Two: RECORD YOUR IDEAS

The second step to brainstorming and opening the closed doors to your creativity is to record your ideas. Have a tape recorder at hand or a journal in which to write down your creative thoughts. Say or write down what you believe you'd like to do in order to open up your mind to new mental adventures.

This isn't a time to be a critic. Some of your ideas may be profound, while others may be weak, and you may be tempted to discard them right away. But the most significant feature to this step is not to be judgmental or critical of any of the ideas that come to you. Don't get in the habit of writing something down or speaking into a recorder and then erasing or wiping out your thoughts. I've found through experience that we can be our own worst critics. For this creative exercise, I'd like you to suspend all your critical comments and evaluations, and reserve them for after you've completed your "brainstorming creative list." This isn't the time to be an editor.

It's one thing if you don't like what you've written or said because your gut tells you it's just not right, but it's another thing to disregard any of your ideas because they're different from anything you've thought about before. Keep all of your ideas. You never know when they may come in handy.

Step Three: HAVE FUN WHILE BEING CREATIVE!

Allow yourself to think freely. Don't worry about how wild or freaky your thoughts or ideas are sounding while recording them or writing them down, or relaying them to colleagues or friends. Remember, you're trying to enhance your creative psyche and creativity is always a little out-there at times—or at least it may seem to be to the trained logical mind. What we're trying to do here is to get you thinking out of the box. You, or someone else, has put your current way of thinking into your head. You need to be creative and have some fun to get that straitlaced part of you to loosen up a bit.

When it comes to being creative, peculiar ideas are good. In fact, they're fun! Once you get going, you'll find yourself and whomever you're brainstorming with laughing out loud. You'll surprise yourselves when you see how your thinking morphs, how the stifled way you'd typically think changes, and how interesting your ideas can be once you begin to open the door to creative thinking. How better to find a way to arise to the different, and sometimes odd occasions that come up in our lives than to think a little oddly, too. And you know what? Some really freaky or bizarre ideas can turn out to be the most enjoyable and most practical ways to expand your creative horizons.

Relax Your Energy!

KEY 4

One of the most important keys to unlock the treasure chest of our consciousness is Key 4—"R." But ironically, the key that is so valuable to our instinctive growth is the same key that many people believe to be the most difficult key to maintain. It doesn't have to be that way, and maintain it, you must!

Now, don't start having heart palpitations thinking about maintaining another thing in your already very busy life. Becoming aware and keeping your fourth key sharp is very simple, far from an agonizing psychological task. Brushing your teeth every day isn't an agonizing chore, is it? Of course not. We do so to maintain healthy teeth and gums and to freshen our breath. As we perform this daily responsibility, we don't give it a second thought. Even little children know that it's just something we all have to do every day in order to have a clean, healthy smile. Our smile is a big part of who we are. We use it to greet the world every day, and every day the world sees our smile. And every day, the universe sees how confident or insecure or anxious we are. Don't you want to freshen your confidence the same way you refresh your smile? Of course you do, and you'll be able to do it effortlessly once you're reintroduced to "R."

In order to safeguard and maintain your fourth key, "R," you first have to find the calm place in your center.

My daughter Jackie and I realized this together when one of us was overly anxious about a certain task that we had to undertake. At one time or another, we felt that we didn't have the time or energy to do everything we had to do in a certain time period. What happened? One or both of us "caught an attitude." I would define "catching an attitude" as having nervous or anxious energy. Sometimes Jackie and I could get a little carried away with each other, both being Scorpios. Scorpios, above all, are known for thick-headedness, so we can step on each other's toes even when we have the best of intentions. So Jackie and I can get on each other's nerves when we see things differently. And because we are not only mother and daughter, but we also work together, Jackie and I had to find a way for us to maintain the best working atmosphere that we could.

People don't always agree with each other, and Jackie and I are no different. We have learned that Key 4, "R," is a necessity for us in our everyday lives—not only for us to work and live in harmony with each other, but to live harmoniously with the rest of the world.

My daughter and I realized a long time ago that when we bicker over silly things, the energy around us gets disturbed. Then, the things we need to accomplish that day don't happen, or won't happen, until we unite our energies and calm and relax the vibrations coming from our bodies. And when your energy is calm and relaxed, your attitude will be calm and relaxed.

When you learn how simple Key 4 is to maintain, it will open your instincts to the peace and serenity that will enhance your life. It will unlock all the closed doors and corridors to your dreams.

Like brushing our teeth, relaxing our energy is important to our physical health. Just as we should brush our teeth more than once a day, we should also exercise maintaining a calm energy during the day whenever the going gets a little tense.

So, let's get the show on the road. The road I'm taking you on leads to calm and peaceful energy, where you'll be able to discern who you are and what it is that you actually want from life.

This chapter won't teach you how to acquire your fourth key. There's no need to acquire something you already possess. That's right, you already have your fourth key. The trick is showing you how to stay on the right road so you can connect to your key easily. On this road, you'll find how to embrace the peaceful calm inside of you, which I'm certain some of you believe never existed. This chapter will be your guide in helping you to develop your key and keep it from rusting.

How can the fourth key become rusty? From lack of use. The more anxious and nervous we are, the more rusty our instincts become and the rustier our keys become. This happens every time we fail to access our positive energy so we can relax our inner core, such as when stress enters our lives.

It doesn't take a rocket scientist to understand that the calmer we are, the easier we'll be able to understand our intuition and instincts, and we will also boost our immune systems.

As I mentioned, you already own the key that contains the power of peace and intuition. Yes, even those of you who are known to be Nervous Nellies (someone who is always afraid she made the wrong call or afraid the other shoe is going to drop), and those of you who can't for the life of you imagine that you already possess such a wonderful gift—you do!

With each anxious episode you give in to, you're distancing yourself from your key. You and you alone are making a difficult matter worse by not utilizing your natural ownership of your fourth key—the key that will direct you to always make the right decision for you and for those connected to you. You're the proprietor of the "R" in you and it's there inside you for the taking.

Confidence, Conviction, and Control

There are three essential lessons you will learn about Key 4—"R."
They are confidence, conviction, and control.

CONFIDENCE

When your energy is relaxed and you let go of all your anxieties,
your confidence level rises automatically. This happens not just
within your mind, but also within and around your energy field.
That energy field is felt not only by you, but by the entire universe
because we are all one and connected.

You see, your relaxation makes others aware that you're a confident person. I don't have to remind you that relaxed people are
easy to be around. But I do want to remind you that a person who
maintains a calm and relaxed state of being is destined to make
the best decisions. A tranquil person emanates to all the sense
that "what will be, will be," whatever comes his way during a typi-
cal day. (This doesn't mean that the person radiating that "Que
sera, sera," attitude doesn't care about an outcome.)

A confident or relaxed person may have already found her
fourth key. She may have possessed natural self-assurance and
tranquil energy from birth. Or she may have discovered through
past experiences that Key 4 is how she will get where she wants

to be in life. Or perhaps she had had trouble achieving goals when she was anxious, and made a conscious decision to change her outlook. It doesn't matter how we come to the key. What matters is that we can all unlock the boundaries and doors that cause our instincts and senses to get rusty and out of control.

If you're someone who finds it hard to stay calm when turbulent patches come up in life, pay attention now and just hold on tight to your inner voice, the one that tells you that everything will be okay if only you stay calm and think rationally. Listen to the intuitive you that tells you to fight the temptation to lash out at someone when things don't go exactly as planned. Or, give in to your instincts to be calm so you don't say something out of anxiety that you'll only regret later.

I know I'm making it sound easy, but really, it is. Know this: the first time you use this lesson will be the hardest. All you have to do to recapture your fourth key—"R"—is to learn how to act with confidence rather then react negatively with insecurity.

When you first begin to brush up on your confidence and cultivate a relaxed state of consciousness, you may feel as though as you're being bombarded with anxious decisions. That's just the way the universe helps us sharpen our skills and helps us to keep our keys from rusting. Keep the energy around you relaxed and don't lose faith, and you'll see that a dream that you've waited to come true for what seems like forever, will come true. Your presents will finally arrive.

The universe bestows on you, with your help, everything that you've been praying for. Sure, things were being held up, but that's just because your key wasn't sharpened enough to open the doorway to your rewards.

CONVICTION

When I think of the word conviction, the first synonym that pops into my mind is determination. Our fourth key, "R," will help you understand that if you want to enhance your life, you must try your best with complete conviction and determination that what you want to achieve is within reach. But let's not mix up determination and conviction with the negative "O" word, and that's obsession. Why do I consider obsession to be negative? Because it creates anxious actions, and anxious actions create anxious or negative energy. Therefore your negative energy field will push away what you're determined to achieve.

But if your energy is determined as well as relaxed, and if you work at everything you do with conviction and confidence, there's nothing to obsess or be anxious about. You'll enhance your life the way you've envisioned with peace of mind.

CONTROL

Ah, control. One of the hardest lessons. Control is a part of our natural makeup that is difficult to give up. I know that it's hard for me to allow anyone to handle my affairs. But I've found that while I don't have to give up control of my life to anyone, I am able to relinquish control of some of the maintenance that my life needs to keep running smoothly. I still make all my own decisions and follow my instincts, but I allow others to give me their opinions, and I really do listen.

The negative implication of the word control manifests itself when we feel the need to be in charge of someone else's life. When that happens (and I'm not speaking about underaged children), we're making the statement that we don't trust that person to make his own decisions. Or, we're afraid to let him make his own decision because we might not like his choices. It all stems from our insecurities. When we give up controlling, or trying to control situations we have no right to and that we don't own, we gain control of our senses. Our instincts will be sharper than ever, and we'll never feel insecure again because we'll walk away from any negative situation before it becomes destructive.

Energy

Key 4 is the energy that emanates from our spirit. It's not something you can recharge by drinking one of those new-age energy-boosting concoctions, or by taking a daily vitamin supplement. "R," the acrostic letter used in connection with Key 4, has the purpose of reminding you to relax, or to relax your energy. You have the power to control your actions and to be secure with your life choices. I believe that one of the most potent energy relaxers is our natural gift of visualization that is also integrated in our genetic mix—our DNA.

In fact, just visualizing a need or a want can actually boost physical as well as mental and spiritual energy; not to mention the boost it gives our self-confidence, which in turn relaxes our innate energy. Every time you meditate and visualize a scenario that you wish to integrate in your daily life, you are enhancing your ability to relax your energy field.

Visualization is a very important part of finding success. I love to teach people through visualization. When I ask you to visualize, I'm showing you how my mind actually sees things. I only ask you to visualize what I've already seen. I don't sit back and try to visualize on a certain subject. The visions or scenarios come to me whenever I'm asked a question. The questions are often ones that others would have to sit and contemplate before answering, but my mind or my intuition shows me a visual answer—a scenario. (It's no wonder why I've always had a passion to collect movies and documentaries.)

Some may believe that my mind works differently than most. When a client or a friend asks me a question I don't think about what my verbal response would or should be. That's how a therapist or a psychologist would work, and I am neither. My brain most times presents a visual answer and I attribute that to my instincts being at work. My brain first shows me the big picture, then the verbal lesson follows right behind. Of course there are times that I do receive a whisper or a thought, but in all honesty I most frequently receive a virtual DVD version of what the outcome, procedure, move, or direction would be to a question presented to me.

When you visualize, you can get closer to reaching your instincts and relaxing your energy. To put it simply: if we are anxious, insecure, obsessive, or just plain used to whining about anything that doesn't go our way, our energy becomes depleted. The likelihood of us enhancing our lives starts to fade. If anyone believes they're a chameleon who can hide their anxieties, self-doubts, or insecurities from the people they're hoping to win over, as they say in Brooklyn, "Fuhgedda-boudit!" You're not a chameleon. You're a Chihuahua, or at least you have the anxieties of a small dog in a great big world.

Everyone can pick up the "Chihuahua" energy. That's right, Chihuahua. Chihuahua energy is the energy of that small dog who will bark and maybe even nip at you if you get too close, or if it's nervous. And Key 4, "R," is really all about how *not* to be a Chihuahua.

Now, if you're a dog, there's nothing wrong with being a Chihuahua. I'm not anti-dog or anti-Chihuahua, for that matter. Chihuahua behavior is okay if you're a dog. As far as I know, dogs don't read books. But they can read you as well as people can. I believe Chihuahuas and other small dogs are so nervous because they know they are small and can be easily hurt by most of the world that they have to look up to. Understandable. But we are not small dogs. We are human beings, and we can be as large and as courageous as our minds. (This makes me think of the saying, "There are no small minds, only minds that do not realize what they are capable of.")

In "Symptoms of Energy" we'll talk in greater detail about what it means to be a Chihuahua, and what a mess Chihuahua energy can mean for a relationship.

The Akashic Field

Relaxing your energy is an absolute must if you want to enjoy your life. You cannot enhance your life if you're not happy or at least en route to happiness. If you're trying to make your life better, you must do so with a positive outlook and without bitterness for what you've gone through in the past. You have to give up any thoughts of resentment, jealously, and envy, and allow yourself to learn from the past, not live in it. We can do that by learning more about the ancient belief called "Akashic Record," or "Askashic Field."

The term Akashic Field comes from an eastern term for a planetary recorder. That's right, it's more or less a DVD of planetary history. This recorder, or recorder cell, as it's sometimes called, is believed to keep track of everything in our planet's history, from actual happenings to the feelings of those who inhabit the planet. When we're connecting to our Akashic Field, we are in essence connecting with the electromagnetic and gravitational force of the planet. Energy bands are able to record the information of our consciousness, which cannot be ignored, dismissed, or erased, no matter how hard our subconscious tries to bury it.

The Akashic Field teaches us that every one of us has a place of our own in our spirit, where our collective and individual memories are stored. The theory of the Akashic Field is that we are the sum of all that we've experienced in our past.

I can see you tapping your finger on the page or on your temple, wondering, "What does learning about the Akashic Field have to do with enhancing my present or future happiness?" Well, I'm sure you've heard people say, "I've learned from my past mistakes." Well, that statement is truer than you know. We really can learn how to connect to our past, or connect to our past mistakes, by tapping into our Akashic Field.

When I give a person a reading about her future on the radio, when I don't get to see her face and she cannot see mine, I usually pause. I'll tell listeners that the silence they're hearing for a moment is just my meditating on the caller's past, in order for me to find the best path for her future. In essence, I'm connecting with her Akashic Field. When we learn how to relax our energies, everyone can connect with their Akashic Field. You may not be able to connect, as I or other intuitives do, with a stranger's A.F., but you'll be able to read your own. (To succeed, though, you'll have to get rid of that Chihuahua energy or nervous energy.)

The Akashic Field is a subtle communication that connects everything to everything else in the universe, regardless of distance, time (distance between our past and our present lives), or separation (example, when I'm reading someone over the radio or phone that may be calling me from Australia). The separation of two people means nothing to the universe and doesn't stand in the way of our ability to read a person's Akashic Field.

When we learn how to relax and meditate properly, we can instantaneously be taken back to another time in our life. It may be a time similar to one we're in now. Maybe we're about to make a mistake that we made once in the past. We can recall at once the recordings of our life where the crossroads were similar, but this time, we can choose to make a right turn instead of the left turn we made in the past. When we realize we're capable of doing all that for ourselves, our self-esteem is at its highest level and we can't be unhappy for long. That's as long as you've really listened to your past and learned by it, and you've embraced it all with peace and unwavering faith that everything will turn out as it should—with the most positive outcome.

Understanding and practicing Key 4, "R," is imperative to you and your happiness. I've found in my years as a professional intuitive that too many people have gotten used to being unhappy with their lives. They're truly unaware that they're showing others their energy is not relaxed, that they're insecure and anxious, and that they have no faith in themselves or their future. Yip yip. That's right. It's the Chihuahua energy again. (Make sure you read "Symptoms of Energy.")

There may be times when you find yourself in a continuous state of conflict. Times when the world and everyone in it seem to be on a different page or path then you are. You can correct it. Take a step back out of your life for a moment or two and take a good look at what's going on in your life—from the outside looking in. Why is your boss out of sorts with you? Why are your children misbehaving like they never have before? Why is your health on the decline? Try your best to be completely objective.

Your Energy and Your Health

Some people who do not know how to relax their energy have, or may have been recently diagnosed with, fibromyalgia or chronic fatigue syndrome (CFS). The medical definitions are as follows:

Fibromyalgia is a debilitating chronic illness characterized by diffuse pain, fatigue, and a wide range of other symptoms. It is a syndrome, not a disease. It is not contagious, and appears to have a genetic component. It affects more women than men, mostly between ages twenty and fifty. It is seen in 3 to 10 percent of the general population.*

*Source: http://bone-muscle.health-cares.net/fibromyalgia.php

Approximately 80 percent of chronic fatigue syndrome patients have an overlapping diagnosis of fibromyalgia syndrome, which includes persistent muscle pain. To the vast majority of sufferers, CFS and fibromyalgia are the same illness.

More than 800,000 people in the U.S. alone are estimated to suffer from chronic fatigue immune dysfunction syndrome (CFIDS), and between 60 and 85 percent of CFS cases are women. Fibromyalgia syndrome is easier to diagnose and affects more than 5 million Americans, 87 percent of them women. The symptoms of chronic fatigue syndrome and fibromyalgia are said by one study to be caused by a combination of four factors: loss of healthful sleep patterns, hormone imbalances, opportunistic infections, and nutritional deficiencies.

Another study reports:

Fibromyalgia has been characterized as musculoskeletal aches and pains that manifest in several tender points throughout the body. Fibromyalgia remains a medical mystery even to this day. The pain in the muscle can have a constant ache or twitch and may even burn at times. Pain is predominantly the most common complaint from most fibromyalgia sufferers. Pain may start in one area and over time spread throughout the entire body. *

*Source: Felicitas Jugulion, MD, Jesse Alex Juguiion, MD, Christian Martin, RPS-GT, "Analysis from afar," in *Sleep Review, The Journal for Sleep Specialists*, July/August 2007.

Why, you may ask, am I giving you so much clinical information with regard to a medical condition in a book on how to awaken your instincts and enhance your life?

Because I believe as an intuitive, and as someone who was also diagnosed with this syndrome over twenty years ago, that stress and the lack of relaxation are the main culprits. My diagnosis came coincidentally, around the same time as the major crossroads in my life, while I was under the tremendous stress of working two jobs and raising three children as a single parent. That's why I believe I was diagnosed with the syndrome (and this is my opinion and not that of a medical physician).

Because this condition now affects five million Americans, 87 percent of whom are women, I think it is necessary to talk about it. When I looked for help, some doctors looked at me as though I had two heads, or at best considered me a hypochondriac. So if you're also looking for help, I want you to be well-armed with some facts, to know you're not the only one suffering these symptoms.

I fully believe that over the years, the stress, some of which I helped cause myself, just took its toll on my body. My body eventually said, "Hey, I can't take anymore!"

Don't Allow a Diagnosis to Define You!

We've talked about how the keys can help you improve your physical health as well as your mental health. You also need to understand how you can rise above an illness, and not let the diagnosis define you.

When I was first disabled with MS, I looked at a lot of self-help books. I tried reading everything to heal myself and to get my head pointed in the right direction. I can honestly say that while I found good direction in some, most of the books didn't speak to me where I lived. They weren't written by someone who had been there and back. I felt like Alice in Wonderland stuck in the rabbit's hole, with the rest of what we call the "normal world" I once knew turned upside down. The books I was reading seemed to be for people who were literally, physically, and metaphorically, still standing right side up.

Out of all the reading I've done and the lessons I've learned in my thirty-five years of being an intuitive, my daughter Jackie was one of my best teachers. This was when she was just five years old—the year I was diagnosed with multiple sclerosis. You see, Jackie never saw me as ill or diseased. When asked by her classmates what it was like having a mother who was so sick, Jacqueline's reply was, "My mother's not sick, she's just resting until she can get better." And she was right. Jackie taught me through her words and actions that I shouldn't allow myself or the rest or the world to define me by my diagnosis.

A chronic disease can impact not only how others see you but how you see yourself. An article in *The Journal of Advanced Nursing* (Vol. 34, No. 3, May 2001) states that chronic illness—defined as an illness that causes a disruption of life—causes identity transformation among women with chronic fatigue syndrome and fibromyalgia.

People with chronic illnesses often suffer from identity loss. Research concerning patients with chronic fatigue syndrome (CFS) or fibromyalgia has not, however, adequately addressed consequences of these illnesses for identity. This *Journal of Nursing* article describes how the women with CFS and fibromyalgia create new concepts of identity after the onset of their illness.

Now, I don't want to address just one illness or syndrome. Whatever your malady, if you have any identifying transformations, you cannot succumb. You can't let any kind of medical, physical, or emotional diagnosis allow you to feel that you somehow cannot have awakened instincts or that you can't attain the keys.

You may be someone who has been under an enormous amount of stress and you've found yourself not feeling well physically. Or, you may have recently received a medical diagnosis that makes you fear that you'll never be able to reach your unreachable star in life. Get that thought out of your head this very minute. You can overcome anything today using conventional medical procedures mixed with the unconventional, such as natural healing remedies that your nutritionist may recommend, as well as using your natural instinct, which gives you the key to sense your body's needs.

Medical Intuition

I've got some wonderful news for you. You are your best doctor and your best medical intuitive!

Now, hold on . . . I'm not telling you that you don't need to see a physician or go for a yearly medical check-up. What I'm saying is that you can help your doctor diagnose you if and when you learn how to read your own body, as only you can. No one knows you better than you. I've learned as a medical intuitive that most of the time people with less-than-perfect physical or emotional conditions are the most eager to learn. They have a true craving to experience a spiritual enlightenment as a way to awaken their instincts, more so than those who have been healthy all of their life.

For those of you who have always been healthy, this does not mean that you cannot read your body as well as anyone else. It could very well mean that you've been healthy *because* you have been reading your body, mind, and spirit so well for so long that you're in perfect harmony already. If that's so, hats off to you! But for those of you who have been healthy courtesy of sheer DNA, and who feel you really don't have a clue about what's going on inside your body, well, the wait is over! You now have this book as your tool to reconnect with yourself on every level.

Two Tips for "Relaxing Your Center"

As I've said, a big part of staying healthy in general is being able to relax the energy around you. You first need to recognize what's destabilizing the energy in your vicinity. If you can see the causes of the anxious energy, you'll be able to relax your core and there-fore, be able to enhance your life and every aspect of it for once and for all.

Tip 1: MAKE A LIST

Make a short list of conscious choices. Make a list of things about yourself and your daily routine that make you anxious and that you're not too thrilled with. I'm sure you can come up with a few, such as being nervous around your boss, getting stressed when you're faced with meeting new people, or feeling anxious if you have to tell someone you disagree with them.

Before you start your list, make a conscious choice to calm and relax your energy or your chi, the vital force believed in Taoism and other Chinese thought to be inherent in all things. The unimpeded circulation of chi and a balancing of its negative and positive forms in the body are believed to be essential to good health in traditional Chinese medicine. Free-flowing and balanced chi will help you to have more patience with everyone else, as well as with yourself. You can refer to your list as you choose which part of your behavior you wish to change first.

Tip 2: LEARN TO MEDITATE OR LISTEN TO MEDITATION CDS

People may tell you to get rid of stress and chill out a little. Their intentions may be good, but you're going to get even more stressed as you worry about their instructions to you. So here's a worry-free stress breaker you can try—even if you're not by nature a meditation lover.

When I tell people to meditate in order to help themselves relax, most of the time I hear lots of moans in the background. Why? Many people who truly try to meditate on their own say it doesn't work because they keep losing track of what they were or weren't supposed to be doing. Or, they become distracted when they're supposed to be relaxing. Makes sense, right?

My advice to everyone, no matter what your age or gender, is to find a good meditation CD, put it in your portable CD player, and carry it with you at all times. If you own an iPod you can download one of your favorite meditation CDs and meditate on your way to work instead of listening to music.

Or, you can pop an earpiece in your ear before you go to bed to relax your entire body as well as your mind so you truly get a good night's sleep. I don't measure a good night's sleep by how many hours you've slept. A good night's sleep, I believe, should be measured by how you've increased your awareness through relaxation, as well as how much you've strengthened your immune system.

We have known for some time that stress affects our immune systems. Many studies have shown that stress can suppress the immune system, but other studies have shown boosts in the immune system under stress. A July 2004 analysis of 293 studies conducted over the past thirty years puts the pieces of the puzzle together. Psychologists Suzanne Segerstrom, PhD, and Gregory Miller, PhD found the following:*

- Stress does indeed affect the immune system in powerful ways.
- Short-term stressors boost the immune system.
- It seems that the "fight or flight" response prompts the immune system to ready itself for infections resulting from bites, punc-

*Source: Suzanne C. Segerstrom and Gregory E. Miller, "Psychological stress and the human immune system: a meta-analytic study of 30 years of inquiry," *Psychological Bulletin*, Vol. 130(4) 2004.

tures, scrapes, or other challenges to the integrity of the body.
• Chronic, long-term stress suppresses the immune system.

The longer stress endures, the more the immune system shifts from the adaptive changes seen in the "fight or flight" response to more negative changes, first at the cellular level and later in broader immune functions. The most chronic stressors—those that seem beyond a person's control or seem endless—resulted in the most global suppression of immunity. Chronic stress causes almost all measures of immune system function to drop across the board.

You can see why it's imperative for us to learn to relax in order to stay healthy and maintain a wonderful quality of life. I have created my own meditation CD, entitled "Connecting to Heaven's Gate," that explains how to connect to your first five senses before your try to connect to your sixth, and also helps you with visualization.

I created my CD not only for adults, but also for children, to help them relax before they go to sleep at night or before they're about to take a (hopeful) daytime nap. Many parents have told me they find themselves falling asleep listening to it with their children. My meditation CD isn't the only one on the market. There's a large selection to choose from. I strongly suggest that you consider purchasing whichever one you choose for your kids too, because your children's need for relaxation may be even greater than yours. And remember, a happy relaxed child makes for a happy relaxed parent!

Before I leave my house every morning, I make sure to meditate and allow my natural senses to awaken with me so I can be in the right mental zone, not only for my day, but for my job on my radio show.

I have a huge collection of meditation tapes and CDs, but when I just need to connect to the universe, I prefer to listen to Gregorian chant.

What's Gregorian chant? As defined by Wikipedia (the free online encyclopedia), Gregorian chant is the central tradition of Western plain chant, a form of monophonic, unaccompanied sacred songs of the Roman Catholic Church. (You certainly don't have to be Catholic to enjoy the chanting of the monks, though it does sound as though you're reaching heaven with their voices!) Gregorian chant developed mainly in Central Europe during the ninth and tenth centuries, with later adaptations. Popular legend credits Pope Gregory the Great with inventing Gregorian chant.

So when you're looking for meditation CDs, sample some of the monks' work, or give any other one a try. Keep looking until you find one you like, and then use it!

Never Say Never

KEY 5

I'd like to share with you a poem I wrote two decades ago, back in 1987. The poem, entitled "Against All Odds," was written at one of the lowest points in my life. Yet looking back now, from a brighter, healthier, and a much more positive end of life's spectrum, I realize there were good things that came out of that year. Although the year held many painful changes and demanded frightening decisions for me, it was also the year that squeezed out the hidden passions I had for life that I was too busy whining and worrying about to cherish.

Jackie was leaving the security of her father's home, with its four bedrooms, large backyard, and an in-ground pool. Of course she was too young to cast her vote as to whether or not we should move, but when I did make the choice to move out and onward, so did she. She was and is my little trouper, never complaining about her new surroundings. In fact, Jackie found it all to be a great adventure. Watching her grow with that type of an attitude over the years enhanced my beliefs in Key 5—"N," which is short for Never Say Never.

I appreciate the value of those life lessons today because I know that without feeling the pain and emptiness of my then-reality, I most certainly would not have found my center and the core of who I am today. Now I know what I am capable of accomplishing, mentally, medically, and spiritually.

Over the years I've come to understand that sometimes, well, most times, we all need a real good kick in the pants in whatever way the universe or God sees fit. That kick will help to emotionally or physically awaken instincts that we have unconsciously disregarded, or taken for granted. Sometimes we actually forget that these instincts exist within us.

That was the year I have etched in my mind as my year of rebirth and the beginning of my awakening. Every tear I shed getting to the point of awareness that I now embrace so eagerly, came with a new life journey that I would carry with me forever. And with every new journey and accomplishment came a smile. There's no greater gift to your soul than the sight of your own face beaming back at you, subconsciously congratulating you on another job well done!

Today, when I think of a smiling face, I'm reminded that smiles symbolize more than happiness and gratification. Your smile represents the beginning of one of those little miracles that you've been waiting for. A miracle is what I was waiting for in 1987, and my memory of the day I composed that poem is still as crystal clear as if I wrote each stanza yesterday.

That year was most definitely one of the main reasons, if not *the* reason, for the substantial turning point as well as learning point, in my life. I learned that I could handle whatever circumstance came my way, be it magnificent or a tumultuous psychological windstorm, and I could still stand tall. I acquired Key 5—"N."

Armed with my new key, I found a new fortitude and awareness, thanks to the powerful life lessons the universe sent my way. Fortunately, I was a willing student of the cosmos. I listened intensely to my instincts and I learned to say and believe with conviction that I should never say never again to anything that my soul might want or desire.

And so, more than twenty years ago, the universe showed me the path to the key to never-say-never-land. The universe hands us nothing. We have to earn whatever we need. The knowledge that came with Key 5 was extraordinary. I did what everyone is supposed to do when they receive a key—I looked for the door it would open. But this was no ordinary door. Behind this door, I found wondrous knowledge and gifts. And the most valuable gift I retrieved from the opened portal was the certainty that I could be my true self—I would never look back and would always look straight ahead into my future.

As I was awakened to my instincts, I felt an urgency to transcribe the feelings and the lessons I had just been served. And so I composed this poem, "Against All Odds." Its composition was bittersweet because the pain of the new reality that was to be our lives sang out loudly in my soul. The words were forever imbedded deeply in the core of my being. It helped me teach my children—by my actions—how to create their own way of life without fear and with a sense of honor. I hope you receive the same peace and power when you read it as I did when I wrote it.

When I decided to write this poem—hold on, let me back up there. You see, I never consciously decided to write anything that day. I just followed my instincts and let the poem flow through me. As I began to write, I recalled a song I grew up loving, a song that always made me feel empowered—"Different Drum" by Linda Ronstadt.

And, strangely enough, as I was writing this chapter, I received an email from my friend Shelly who lives in San Diego, California. She asked me a question: if I could own one original 45 record from my youth, what would it be? At the time of Shelly's question, I couldn't remember the name of the song, but I did remember the lyrics and who sang it. And after perusing my brain for an entire day, I finally recalled that song's title: "Different Drum."

Woo, I thought to myself, "Different Drum." I hadn't thought of the song in almost forty years. Yet as soon as I read Shelly's question, that song's lyrics floated back into my consciousness like an old friend! I remember driving my family nuts playing that record over and over, until I had to eventually buy another copy because the first record got so scratched from overuse. I must have sung the lyrics at least a thousand times. Now, as I find myself singing the song once again, I realize that the song was something of a premonition of my life to come. The last chorus is the part that always touched my soul the deepest.

So good-bye, I'll be leavin'.
I see no sense in this cryin' and grievin'.
We'll both live a lot longer
If you live without me.

And today as I sit in front of my computer and think of the thirteen-year-old girl who sang that song until her voice was hoarse, shivers run down my spine. I find myself pondering if my singing that song created the life I now have, that of a single parent living on her own—happily, I'd like to add. Was it a premonition of a life to come? I think it may be a little of both. I believe that song helped define my beliefs about what kind of love I'd accept in life, and shaped the realization that I would have the strength to live alone if I had to.

So on July 1, 1987, as I marched to the beat of a different drummer, and I unpacked our moving boxes for what seemed like three hours straight, I remember telling myself to take a break for a minute. I plopped down on the nearest chair and looked at the mess that still lay ahead of me. As I glanced around the living room, my glance landed on the unopened box that was next on my list. Suddenly I received an instinctive nudge to open that box right away. So I did. On top of the stack in the box was a black marbled composition notebook that I had used as a journal. I picked it up, found a pen, and went back to my chair. As I opened the notebook and found a blank page, these are the words that poured from my soul:

Against All Odds

I had a title, and then I continued to write until the poem was complete. I remember the words coming to me in one quick swoop, as if guided by a higher power or a super subconscious. And as I wrote, I dug deep inside my soul and instincts to find the words.

I somehow intuitively knew I would read them over and over again during my life when I might be feeling low again. Or, I'd read them when I'd begin to believe those telepathic messages I was receiving from others—messages that said my dreams were just too big and that I should settle for whatever life threw my way. That I should be grateful for whatever crumbs the universe might scatter toward me.

Well, crumbs weren't good enough for me then and they're certainly not good enough for me now.

And I hope this prayer-like poem will also help you believe in your dreams, and that you'll never say never to any of your hopes, dreams, or desires, whether they be for romance, business, health, or anything your heart may desire.

I'm not suggesting you must go it alone, and you can, but you may be able to repair your relationship. I want you to remember that yes, some romantic relationships may fizzle out and die like a sparkler on the Fourth of July, and some couples may grow in different directions and decide to go their separate ways. But, there are those special few whose relationships can start over and wind up even better than before.

Please keep in mind that as long as you still have love in your heart for each other, it's not too late to start again. And don't be afraid. Remember, this book is all about giving up your fears. Sometimes love seems to diminish over the years, but where love exists, no matter how hidden it may be, or how dormant it's been lying, it can be rekindled if you're both unafraid to begin again.

There's one very important thing that you both must do in

order to even begin to think about making a go of it again. You both must promise to let go of past mistakes. Learn from them, of course, but never throw them in each other's faces, no matter what hurts either of you have encountered from each other. If you can do that, and I know it can be done, then and only then, anything and everything is possible.

But for those of you who, like me, choose to go it alone, I humbly introduce you to my soul. These are the words written by a woman trying with every ounce of her spirit to be fearless and expectant of life's possibilities and miracles. And so I reverently introduce you to my soul-solution mantra, written in the form of a poem.

AGAINST ALL ODDS

A woman sat with her friends and spoke of days to come.
She said, Someday I'll be happy.
I'll find it all alone.
Someone who will love me.
Who'll need not to be shown.

He'll cherish and protect me and
Me, I'll do the same.
I'll not settle for my heart's second-best.
I know I'll win life's game.

Her friends all sat and pondered
Could what she says be true?
Where does she get her dreams from?
Her mind has gone askew?

The woman looked at her guests,
And as though she could read their minds
She said . . .
Against all odds is what you think.
A childish dream you say.
If that is so a child I'll be
Until my dying day.

We all have dreams we believe in.
Of this I believe the most.
So believe in yours if any,
And I'll go on with mine.
But, I'll never change my feelings.
Of this there is no sign.

If life you play like a card game.
If so, I'm Ace's Up.
I'll live my life—Against All Odds
NEVER GIVING UP.

You can see from the ending of the poem, "NEVER GIVING UP," that "never say never" has been my motto for the last twenty years. It's one I've found to be a tremendous help in keeping my keys sharp. It has also helped me to unlock the desires and dreams that were bursting to get out from my soul. And in hindsight, the young teenage girl I was, singing in my attic bedroom to Linda Ronstadt's "Different Drum," learned from the poetry of the music. I was enchanted by the theme and was inspired not to be afraid to dance to a different drummer, or to be independent and to listen to my instincts first and foremost. And most importantly I realized the hard way how the word "never" should never be said when it comes to things on your wish list of life.

The person who said it the best was Muhammad Ali:

Champions aren't made in gyms. Champions are made from something they have deep inside them—a desire, a dream, a vision. They have to have last-minute stamina, they have to be a little faster, they have to have the skill and the will. But the will must be stronger than the skill.

You can emulate Muhammad Ali and the many others who have learned to never say never. Here's how:

Seven Steps to Key 5, or Seven Steps to "N"

1. Never believe that you're not smart enough to learn something new. Make a conscious choice to learn something new every day.

2. Never let anyone else define you or your dreams or your life's plan.

3. Never be afraid to tackle something new and never give up on any dream, wish, hope, or journey, no matter how big or how small. Remember, nothing is too big for you to obtain. All you need is the heart and soul of your dream.

4. Never be afraid to be spontaneous. If it feels good in your gut, then, go for it!

5. Never say yes to something just to be contrary, or just because you've promised yourself to never say never. Always keep in mind that sometimes you might need to say no to someone or something, but that only builds up your dignity and self-esteem. That's not the same as giving up your dreams.

6. Never frown when you have a choice to smile. You might like to try this exercise: Every morning, as you prepare to begin the new day, tell yourself that no matter how rough the day that lies ahead of you becomes, you can weather the storm and wind up with a moonlit evening of peace and tranquility.

7. Lastly, always see the light at the end of the tunnel. That light will lead you to Key 5, which will unlock your door to serenity and success.

Quantum Physics

We've been speaking about things we should never do. Now it's time to change pace and start talking about smart ways to do the things we should do. About dating. Yes, dating tips. My instincts have told me that these tips will be helpful to you, but read carefully before you continue. Ladies, these first tips are just for you. But not to worry, gents, your list will follow right behind.

The purpose of these tips is to enhance your dating life without you ever breaking a sweat or shedding a tear. The really delicious part is that you won't have to follow any rules, or have a complete makeover in order to find the right life partner for you. You won't even become conscious of the changes that are happening to you, but I promise you they'll be painless and joyful. You see, the universe will be taking care of your heart's desires, especially when you put your intentions out there in the atmosphere. Believe me, it works. You'll see it when you have all the dates you can handle and all the choices your heart can handle.

So how will the universe do all this for you? Easy. It's all quantum physics.

What? You say you didn't take physics in school and you're not even good at math or science? Not to worry, my dear friends, because quantum physics is the key here and the ruler of the dating heavens. Here's why. Your behavior and your energy are the same. Everything is energy, and your energy equals your behavior. Your behavior affects, so does your energy. Everything goes out into the universe and becomes you and how everyone sees and feels you. And the universe sees you as someone who's worth the best in life and someone who will not stand for any games when it comes to your heart. Then you'll be in a win-win situation. Finally, after you've realized that the universe not only has eyes and ears, but also has a heart, you'll win at *love* too!

SIX STEPS TO ENHANCE DATING FOR WOMEN

Dating is not a game and these are not rules. These dating steps are meant to enhance a woman's self-respect. And that, in turn, will allow you to enjoy dating without the anxieties and the insecurities many woman feel.

1. Don't obsess about being single. Enjoy your single life and your life's journey.
2. Never ask for a man's number first, ever!
3. Don't be so quick to hand over your phone number, either.

Don't forget your soul and spirit are valuable commodities that shouldn't be given away so easily. And don't give a strange man too much information about your life.

4. Don't date any of your friends' ex-husbands or ex-boyfriends, ever! This tip is especially important if you know that your friend still has feelings for her ex. However, if she gives you the go ahead, it's okay, but only if the two of you have talked about it openly first. Remember, boyfriends may come and go, but a good friend will last a lifetime!

5. When you do exchange numbers with a new man and you've begun dating, return his calls casually. Never call him back immediately after he's called you unless it's an absolute emergency. (And ladies, don't make up an emergency. It's got to be a real emergency.)

6. Think like a man, but act like at woman. It's easy, girls! Just think like a caveman in a dress!

Yes, I said a caveman in a dress. I'll never forget what drove this viewpoint home for me. I was dating someone I was crazy about many years ago. The man told me in jest that I shouldn't worry about how he felt about me if he didn't call when he promised. He said I shouldn't worry because I was safely on the top of his "top ten list." Lucky me!

At that precise moment something snapped in my consciousness, but in a good way. From that day forward, I realized I had to start keeping a mental dating list of my own, just like most men do. Not a list created out of revenge or because I felt angry, but because my instincts made me feel it was the right thing to do. And, as an intuitive explorer of consciousness, I figured 40 percent of the single male population dated just one person at a time. And although I'm not great at math, I believe that leaves us with a whopping 60 percent of the rest of the single hunks out there on the dating scene who have a list of women they date. Many have an actual notebook of the girls that they are dating, in order of their favorites. Something like David Letterman's Top 10 List.

So ladies, unless you've been given an actual engagement ring (and I'm not being materialistic here), or unless the two of you have put down a deposit on a church or a reception hall for your future wedding, keep on dating!

A very important note here: I'm not telling women to be promiscuous. I'm only telling women to have more than one male friend at a time, and they don't have to be physical relationships. You can go for coffee, brunch, dinner, a movie, to play golf, or to see a baseball or football game. You can do lots of things in public, or things that aren't too intimate, with the lights on. These are the things you can also tell your mother about after a date while you're dating more than one man.

And the minute you start thinking like a man—dating-wise, that is—your whole dating experience is going to change. You see, men enjoy dating and most of them consider every date another conquest.

When women date, it's a whole other ball game. Most women feel they have to *endure* dating if they're ever going to find Mr. Right, the man they'll wind up marrying. Most women are uncomfortable dating more than one man at a time. But once a woman realizes that she can have fun dating more than one person, she'll finally be able to relax and enjoy it without worrying about stepping on anyone's toes.

SEVEN STEPS TO ENHANCE DATING FOR MEN

OK, guys, don't take insult at these steps. There's nothing wrong with having a good time, but if you want to enter a serious relationship, this is the way to go.

1. Treat a nice girl right! If you believe you're ready to date seriously and you want to find someone who can be in tune with you both mentally and physically (not just someone you will lust for), don't take a nice girl for granted. If you tell her you're going to call her or see her, follow through, or at least don't say anything you don't mean. What do I mean

by a nice girl? She's the girl you felt a special something for the first minute you laid eyes on her. She's a knockout, she's very secure and she doesn't need you to make her feel secure. A nice girl is someone who is morally conscious of her behavior and has loads of integrity.

2. If you're not feeling the same emotions for the girl you're dating as you think she is feeling, or that she's demonstrated by her words and deeds, let her know. She can handle it. Girls won't break. It's better for your karma to be honest, and then you can both go your separate ways. And speaking of karma, gentlemen, never, ever just stop calling a person you've been dating if you believe the relationship just won't work. If the chemistry's not there, be a man and tell her in as friendly a way as possible. Remember, your karma will either kick you or kiss you. You decide which one you want.

3. Don't be afraid to be an old-school kind of guy when it comes to who pays for what on the first few dates. Be the gentleman and pay for the date. Once you two become an item, you can go dutch if you choose to. It's really a good idea, whenever possible, for the gentleman to pick up the woman for the date, instead of meeting her at the place you've chosen.

4. If the woman you've just begun to date is a knockout and she knows that you're crazy about her, that's fine, as long as she never asks to borrow money from you. I would suggest

you follow what I call Mary's rule: "Never lend or borrow money from a friend or romantic partner unless you're co-habitating."

5. Never open a bank account or a checking account together unless you're married to each other!

6. Never become too possessive of each other and never ever check each other's emails or voicemails. And please don't put your new friend's cell phone on your account. That's just a sure way to break up sooner.

7. After you've dated your new person for a month or six weeks, and if you believe this may be the ONE, bring her to meet your parents. Don't go to get their approval, but their opinion. You may not agree with their opinions, but I assure you that if anyone in your family tells you they have a bad feeling around your new friend, listen up. If you don't, you may be very sorry later.

Relationship Questions You Should Ask Before You Leap

Welcome back ladies (okay, I know you read the guys' tips, too). Here are some questions both men and women should consider before any new relationship reaches more serious levels.

TIPS ON HOW TO CHOOSE THE BEST MR. OR MS. RIGHT!

1. What's the first question a woman should ask the new man in her life? "How well do you get along with your family, especially your mother?" A woman should also notice the way her new man speaks about his family, and again, specifically about his mother, when he thinks no one is paying attention. I believe in that old saying my mother told me, and her mother told her: "If a man is good to his mother, he'll be good to you!" And boy, let me tell you, time and time again that old saying has been proven to be true. And yes, you should also be concerned if he's *too* good to his mother. By that I mean if he allows his mother to control his life. If that's the case, end the relationship and thank your lucky stars you're missing out on all the drama that would have followed.

2. The first question a man should ask a woman he's just started dating is: "What do you want from life with regard to your career or education?" Gentlemen, if she shrugs her shoulders and then follows with, "I really haven't given it much thought," be very careful. You could be dating someone who's just looking for someone to make her a "Sadie" (a married lady). Ladies, don't take offense at this, but I must be objec-

tive about both genders. I read both sexes professionally and just because I'm a woman, it doesn't mean I can't give a man good advice, too. And gentlemen, if you want your wife to be a stay-at-home mom, there's nothing wrong with that. In that case you should tell her, so if it's not part of her plan, she'll know where you stand. I believe you should know from the get-go what a woman wants from life.

3. Does your new prospective mate still have a close relationship with his or her ex? If so, that's fine if it's because they have a child or children together—that is, as long as neither of them is still in love with the other. Being mature, kind, loving parents who choose not to be mean to each other, but instead embrace the beautiful human beings they've made together is a good thing. It could be a problem if they discuss your relationship with each other, or if either one of them ever crosses the emotional line into your relationship.

If, however, your new partner has never been married and does not share a child with his or her ex-love, yet they are still very friendly, be very careful. Now, I'm not saying people cannot be friends after they break up. But they can't be calling each other constantly, either. And, if you find that your new love is still calling his or her old love daily, then there's still a fire burning in their hearts for each other. I don't care how many times they swear to you that it's over between them, it isn't.

4. Listen closely to the questions your new date-mate asks you on your first few outings together. If he or she asks you how much money you make, or, whether you rent or own, run for the hills! Why? Asking such private questions about your income and your financial portfolio, well, I'll say five will get you ten that they're a slacker who's looking for an easy ride. If these questions do come up on your first dates, make them your last dates.

5. Does he or she whine or seem to constantly have something negative to say about someone they know or people they've never even met while you're trying to have a normal conversation with them? Negativity begets negativity and nothing good can come from it. If you really like this person, you should make them aware of their negative comments and ask them to try to be more positive with their way of thinking. Then give it a while and see if they've learned how to be more harmonious with the Universe. If after a few weeks you find they haven't changed their negativity yet, or they haven't even tried to look at the brighter side of life, then move on to a more positive person. Remember, people are

usually trying to be on their best behavior in the beginning of a relationship. If negativity is their best in the beginning, just think about what kind of a person they may morph into down the road. I'm visualizing the Wicked Witch of the West.

Dream Yourself into Your Most Perfect Future

When you read a self-help book and the writer starts discussing dreams, you probably think you're going to be shown how you can manifest your long-lost desires and, yes, dreams.

Well, clear your mind of that concept right here and now. From this lesson on, know "Dreaming Yourself into Your Most Perfect Future" is not about manifesting anything that you don't already own.

In this lesson, you're going to learn how to read and interpret your *intuitive* dreams. Yes, the ones that reach you while you're fast asleep in bed—not the daydreams or hopeful plans you have for your future. And in learning how to read and interpret your dreams, you'll be able to make those other dreams, the wishes for the future, happen earlier in your life rather than later.

So how can one lesson and a few quick tips do so much in so little time? It's because these tips will help guide you and teach you how to read the symbols that you are receiving in your sleep every time you close your eyes. Symbols about your future, or should I say, your clairvoyant future. The future you can see even with your eyes shut tight while you're having a regular run-of-the-mill—or so you may believe—actual dream.

Once you realize that you have the key to your sixth sense safely tucked away in your pillow, your life will never be the same again. You'll look forward to sleeping more than ever before, not just for the sake of getting some much needed rest, but because you'll be finding out new information about yourself.

These psychic, informative dreams come to us every time our subconscious is resting comfortably, aligned perfectly with the rest of our senses, which of course includes the sixth sense. Your sixth sense—your intuition—is sending you vital information for your future and your present life every time your brain enters the REM state of sleep. When you're too busy to see what your sixth sense is trying to show you, your subconscious mind says, "Hey, listen up." We dream of things we need to understand.

These intuitive dreams don't only come to sleeping adults. They also come to children every time they put on their p.j.'s and say nighty-night to the outside world. I've found that children are much more perceptive than most adults, so please heed what your children are saying about their dreams. Oh, of course not every dream a child has—or an adult has, for that matter—will be a premonition dream, but once you learn how to interpret the difference, life will become so much less complicated and much more fun too!

These simple tips will help guide you, and direct your children, to become aware of your and their true potential. In addition, your clairvoyant dreams will in fact show you your hidden desires. All you need to do, literally, is go to sleep and dream a little dream to find them. You see, your sleepy-time dreams are nature's way of getting your undivided attention and making you aware that you need not be taught how to make things happen. Why? Because your future is already in your proverbial cards, and now all you have to do is to learn how to interpret your dreams.

DREAM LESSON ONE

In order for you to have a clear-seeing intuitive mind while you're sleeping, make sure before you go to bed that you're calm and relaxed. If you were at odds during the day with anyone in your family or even a close friend, you should make nice before you go to bed. Don't be concerned about who was right or wrong. Kiss, hug, or make a phone call and bring peace to the situation. We need to make peace with our personal world in order for us to create the calm necessary to receive the vital intuitive information that we seek. In addition, your anger and argumentative essence will follow you in your sleep and will mentally influence your intuitive dreams. That negative or disruptive energy will make it impossible for you to understand and decipher your awakened subconscious instincts.

DREAM LESSON TWO

Before you turn in for the evening, burn (for only a few minutes) a stick of Jasmine incense. If you don't have Jasmine, you can use whatever incense you have on hand. Jasmine is my favorite because I find the scent, inhaled ever so lightly before I go to sleep, relaxes not only my mind. It allows my entire body to become one with its bouquet of soothing energy, so that my instincts are automatically enhanced. With your incense in hand, walk around your entire house or apartment. Put the incense in an ashtray or dish as you make your rounds, to make sure you don't burn yourself or anyone or anything while carrying it. At the very least, spread the aroma's calming essence throughout every bedroom.

DREAM LESSON THREE

Keep a journal or a pad and something to write with next to your bed. If you really want to get into exploring your intuition like a scientist, keep a recorder next to your bed. Make sure you give yourself a mental suggestion before you hit the sack that you should wake up when your intuition or your instincts are trying to give you a message. Don't worry about losing sleep because you're trying to track down your intuitive dreams. You only need to stay awake for a few seconds at most. I find myself recording my thoughts with my eyes closed and I don't even remember getting up in the middle of the night. I'm only sure I recorded my thoughts when I turn on my recorder the next day and hear whatever word or phrase I thought was necessary for my guidance.

Keep in mind that many great inventors, artists, movie directors and screen-writers, as well as major entrepreneurs, have said that they've received their best inspiration and guidance through their dreams.

DREAM LESSON FOUR

Dreams will offer symbols that often need a little interpreting. For example, if you've had a dream about an office, it doesn't necessarily mean the office represents your business office. It may represent your need for a new job in a new office, and it's the way your psychic consciousness is telling you that it's time to look for a new office. If you follow through on that, the odds are that you'll find the job or the career of your dreams.

The trick to deciphering this kind of intuitive dream, or any dream for that matter, is that you should always, and I mean always, mentally request that your subconscious (while you're still asleep) clarifies and helps you understand exactly what your intuition is trying so desperately to tell you. Never believe that it's impossible for you to request your subconscious to follow your commands. You're controlling yourself, not anyone else, and as always you are in charge of every part of you. If it doesn't happen the first night, don't give up, because it's like your mother always told you: Anything done well doesn't come by chance—it comes with practice!

DREAM LESSON FIVE

Look for key words or images in your dreams to help you decipher the meaning of your dream. What are your key words?

One key word or image may be your feet. Here's an example: In your dream, your feet aren't touching the ground, and you see yourself levitating or floating about six inches above the ground. A dream like this, which is very common, means to me that you're learning to float and look at yourself from all angles. It also tells me that you're most definitely reaching for a higher vibratory level and that your instincts are awakening. You may even be on the road to an out-of-body experience.

Another key word or image can be eyes. You may see yourself wearing glasses, which may be your body's way of telling you that you need an eye exam, or a new prescription. It could also mean that your eyes need more rest or that you may need to get a pair of glasses or contacts.

Your subconscious has put those key words and/or images in your dreams for you to find and see. As an intuitive, and as someone who has been tracking her own intuitive dreams for more than thirty-five years, I know those keys and images are there for you to find. I taught my daughter Jackie to do it successfully, and I know your intuitive keys are there for the taking. And you know what's so cool about the whole thing? You put the key and the images in your subconscious on your own without the help of anyone else. You know what you need, and you know what your future can hold. We were all born knowing, and our dreams are our gift from the universe to help us treasure hunt for our psychic surprises.

DREAM LESSON SIX

Sometimes your subconscious may use an archetype in your dream. According to Carl Jung, archetypes are an inherited pattern or thought or symbolic image, part of humanity's "collective unconscious." They also manifest themselves in subconscious thoughts and dreams. For example, a "mother figure" is an archetype. The way I see it, when we dream of an archetype, we're being shown what we actually want or need, or what we're meant to be in life. For example:

- You may be directed to become an authority figure or a leader.
- You may be directed to become a healer and find yourself enrolling in classes to train for work doing anything in the medical field.
- Or, you may be directed to become a financial advisor and wind up becoming a financial wizard because that's what you were always meant to be. All you ever needed was the self-assurance that your intuitive dream gave you.

However you're directed by your dreams, listen and take heed because these intuitive awakening thoughts are not just possibilities, they are your intuitive fingerprints. Your dreams are your future, and the only question is *when* your dreams will come to pass—not whether you will succeed, because that's a given. You own your dreams and you own your future. So dream a little dream for you and for me!

Twelve Daily Mantras to Enhance Your Life

I keep these twelve mantras, as I've come to call them, in front of me at all times. They're posted on the wall above my computer in my office. So if life is as the universe says it is, and I am you and you are me and we are one, then I pray that they help guide you as they have done me.

I can make things happen!

I say this mantra daily because every day is a new day. With each new day come many new miracles—that is, if only we allow them to happen. In addition, this mantra also helps me know that I'm not alone in this world. When I'm tired, all I have to do is ask God and the universe for a helping hand, and I know that I have the Higher Power in my corner just waiting to coach me and lift me up.

Snap out of it!

I say this to keep myself from feeling stuck or in a limbo situation. Or I say it when things aren't running as easily as I think they should be, and I catch myself feeling sorry for myself. I just tell myself to "snap out of it," a phrase I've loved since I saw the movie *Moonstruck*. Cher's character slaps her fiancé's brother in the face and says that when he tells her he thinks he's falling in love with her. The phrase is a great one to get you going—even without the slap attached to it.

It's okay to want the best for myself.

Repeat this mantra if at any time you feel guilty for wanting the finer things in life, be it a better house, a better career, or just a nicer life. The guilt I subconsciously had came from my Catholic parochial school upbringing. I'm not putting blame on my education, just explaining where I believe I first got the idea in my head that wealth was some kind of a sin. You see, I was taught by Franciscan nuns who took a vow of poverty, and somehow I felt I would be betraying my faith to want things that weren't necessities.

But I was wrong, and I went back and observed my old feelings. I began to realize just how important it is for adults or parents to be aware of what we say in front of our children. We need to ask them how they feel about what they observe, or what they understand about something they've just learned (even if the event or conversation they overheard seems minor to you). We should also discuss with them anything new they encounter. This could be something like learning about a different culture, or hearing a fairy tale that frightens them. As someone who is always trying to read the consciousness of others, I've found that children are reading people all the time without being conscious of it. Therefore, it's necessary for us to explain just what the fairy tale teaches us and that becomes a life-lesson.

Young minds may run away with stories if they have no guidance from adults. They may not realize what a story or tale was supposed to illustrate. Their young minds may—without your input—feel guilty that they have a better life when the children they just learned about may be less fortunate then they. This message is extremely important, no matter how pleasant-sounding a message or story.

Remember that some sensitive children might add a little psychological curve or empathy for a situation or lifestyle they've just become aware of, as I did as a child when the Franciscan nuns taught me about their vows of poverty. Again, I'm not blaming the good sisters for my guilt or subconscious distaste for having more than others. But it showed me how important it is to teach our children about different cultures, different stories, and different spiritual ways of life. We should never forget to add that they have their own treasure chests of desires, so they should never feel guilty if they want to achieve or go beyond the people or stories they have just been introduced to.

I finally realized that it was okay for me to achieve my wants and desires, and I meditated on my life and asked questions of myself many years and many mistakes down the line. I began to see what was in the treasure chest in my soul. Our souls' treasure chests are the wants that we have brought with us from a past life. They are filled with issues and needs and accomplishments, which can be in the form of material or nonmaterial undertakings that we didn't receive in a past life, so our spirit brought them this time around to be fulfilled.

For those of you who are computer savvy, here's an analogy

for how we carry our needs or goals from one lifetime to another. We cut and paste. Imagine and that you've listed your goals for your life right now on a Word document, pressed "save," and then went on with your life, trying to carry out your list. Now, imagine that before you finished completing your tasks, you went onto the next domain, or left the physical world. What your spirit does is press "copy" on your Word document, and then "cuts and pastes" your desires from one lifetime to your new treasure chest in your new physical body.

Recognize the problems surrounding you today and address them before they get out of hand.

This is one of the most important mantras I repeat each day. If we don't recognize problems when they come up during our busy day, we have stopped observing life and we are just coasting to nowhere.

In order to thrive and not just survive, you must be open to change.

This mantra is very important to me also because as I've said many times, I'm only human like everyone else. I say this to remind myself that I'm a mere mortal with faults of my own and even in my own life I cannot be right in every situation. I say this to remind myself that I can ask other people their opinions and if those opinions differ from mine, then I should at least be open to listening, because someone else may have the answer for me this time.

Don't allow your computer to rule your life.

This mantra pertains to everyone in the twenty-first century who uses a computer. We usually turn them on the first thing in the morning (that is, if we ever turned them off the night before) and most of us don't go to bed unless our last email is opened and read. And now there's the Blackberry, which means you no longer have to be at your laptop computer to return emails. There is nowhere we can hide to find silence if the brain needs to sit quietly, without speaking, responding, or negotiating with someone about something. I've made a promise to myself that when I'm with my family, especially my parents and grandchildren, I don't pick up or return emails from my phone. In fact, I shut it down, because the minutes and hours we have with our family cannot be replaced.

Keep your business relationships strictly professional when it comes to the opposite sex.

Not that I get too many offers, but I'm very old-fashioned about mixing business and romance. It may work for some people, but I know for me it was disastrous. If you're having a relationship with someone in the same business, egos can get in the way. Decisions may be made that reflect personal interests that are not necessarily the best ones professionally.

Not everything in life is an emergency, so stop worrying and make time for yourself today.

This mantra is to remind me, as well as you, that life is too short. We have to stop and catch our breath and put our feet up for a few minutes, even though our daily planners are completely full. Not everything is an emergency, and this phrase helps remind me not to become obsessed with work.

Remember, everything in life is negotiable.

This phrase reminds us that if we're having a problem with work, family, children, or just about anything that comes along in a given day, don't get crazy and become irrational. If we remain calm, everything is negotiable and can work out. Maybe things won't always go exactly as we planned, but we can still live with the solution and find a positive ending.

Complete all projects on time and never allow someone else to pick up your slack.

This phrase or mantra is more or less self-explanatory. You never leave your mess or work for someone else to do. And a promise made should always be a promise kept. The only exception would be if you did your absolute best and you needed a little more time to complete a certain task.

> **If you're having a problem with someone, say so and always keep the air clear.**

This mantra is meant to tell me that it's okay to speak your mind. If we speak to each other without arguing or shouting, we never have to worry about holding grudges.

> **Keep open all lines of communication and never think you know it all.**

This mantra will always keep you from being a smarty pants, and it lets you know that you've still got a lot to learn and that no one knows it all.

I recommend that you make up your own mantras or phrases and keep them in plain sight every day. These should be words to keep you positive and on your toes in case you ever get that old feeling that good things only happen to other people and not to you. Remember, never say never to anything positive that could possibly fit into your life, be it love, wealth, health, or just plain old peace of mind.

Take It To The Top

There's another poem that I've carried around with me for the same length of time as "Against All Odds," that I wrote within minutes of the first one.

As an intuitive explorer of consciousness, I am certain that there are many people out there—women and men—who have felt the way I did in my heart and soul the day I wrote this poem. And, as synchronicity might have it, you may be going through something this very moment and this poem may help you find the strength you need. I do not say this with an ego or with the hope of accolades over a well-written verse. I say this as a person who once almost lost all hope, and the universe and God, I believe, wrote these words for me when I was too tired, too weak, and too frightened to think for myself. So this poem belongs to all of us. It's called "Take It to the Top!"

TAKE IT TO THE TOP

Why do I feel the way I do?
Why does it always feel like a trip uphill?

If only the top were in sight—
I'm tired of climbing.

Climbing, reaching, grabbing, scrapping, slipping,
falling—only to start yet another trip.

My only wish is to find a level road in which to plant my
feet. Oh, how wonderful it would feel, walking, not
running, at a steady pace.

Life, I know, has its Ups and Downs.
And, I guess as long as I have downs there must
be ups.

But, why do my downs seem to last so long—
and my ups fade so quickly in a blink of an eye?

Ah, this time I've got a plan.

Next time, when I reach the top—I won't look down.
Why should I?
I know what's there.

This poem is meant for you to realize that we've all experienced down times in our life, times when we may feel we can't stay afloat in the sea of life long enough to enjoy the warmth of the sunshine. But my friends, we can. Do you know why? Because the cream (our soul and our spirit) always rises to the top. So think of yourself as the cream in an old-fashioned glass milk bottle—the kind that the milkman used to deliver to people's doorsteps every morning. I remember the bottles of milk that were delivered to my door when I had my first child. And I always found cream on the top after I opened the bottle cap.

That analogy shows life as it should be. The best in us will always rise above and no matter who tries—be it life, people, or circumstances—no one can hold you down or hold you back. And if for some reason you feel that you can't stay on the top, you're wrong. If that feeling tries to take you over, even briefly, turn on the switch in your brain that enlightens you and reminds you that you should have no fear about sinking. You've been there before and you know you can float. But this time you've learned how to hold onto your life-preserver (your seven keys) and you never need to fear the climb to the top again.

Now that you've opened your consciousness to your daily intention mantras, and now that you more or less understand how to implement the keys that unlock your fears, I believe you're ready for your Daily Questionnaire.

I've designed these questions not to give you agita or anxiety, but to help you rid yourself of it during the course of your day. I recommend you write or type these exact questions so you can have them handy for you to answer before your day begins.

Seven Daily Questions

1. *Are their any fires I have to put out today?* This question can pertain to work, home, or children. This could also remind you to turn off the stove. (I'm not kidding!)

2. *How am I physically feeling today?* As you ask yourself this, move your shoulders up and down and feel the muscles in your neck and upper back. Then, make a mental note about how they feel. If your muscles seem tense, then maybe you're overdoing your time on the computer, or you may be under abnormal stress at work or at home. This question will keep you abreast of your stress levels and get you used to feeling your body before the stress overcomes you.

3. *How is my career going?* When you ask yourself this question, feel what your gut is telling you. Your instincts are in great form in the morning and are always on point. So, if your stomach feels peaceful when you ask yourself that question, then you're doing just fine. If it feels queasy, then ask yourself a few more questions about why or what you can do to make your job and/or career better.

4. *Have I met my "Intention Manifestation Quota" for the week?"* Your "IMQ" is a quota of at least seven personal intentions you'd like to accomplish for the week. You can do one each day if you choose, or seven in one day. Your inten-

tions might be something like these: This week I'll clean out my closets and give away to the needy whatever I haven't worn for the last six months. Or, this week I'll make sure I weigh myself every day and stay away from carbs. This is your intention list—things you choose to manifest—so you can put down whatever you see fit.

5. *Have I said "I love you" to at least seven people today?* You count as one, so now you just have to find six more people. Why? Because when we learn how to express love by saying the words, it is easier for us to be loved by others. Anyway, doesn't it feel great to say "I love you," just for the sake of it?

6. *Have I given my pet (if you have one) a hug today?* If not, then what are you waiting for?!

7. *Are all my bills paid and up to date?* It's a good thing to remind yourself every day about any outstanding obligations. It's not to cause you anxieties, but to keep you from spending money that you really don't have to spend.

Observe the Universe and All That It Holds

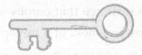

KEY 6

*It is the supreme art of the teacher to awaken joy
in creative expression and knowledge.*

—ALBERT EINSTEIN

Most of us believe that in order for us to observe or examine anything in life, we must do so with our eyes literally opened, but
that's not so. Our intuition doesn't have eyes, and yet we can see
using our mind's eye. We see what our consciousness is making
us feel, and thus our instincts turn what we feel into a vision or
a thought. Now what we were once feeling is like a movie we're
watching on a wide-screen TV in our mind.

Our intuition and instinct allow us to see and observe not only what we're feeling, but the feelings of others, without ever looking up from our desk when we're working. Or feel or observe (without seeing with our eyes) what's going on in our home in the middle of the night without leaving our beds.

We observe reality every minute of our life, whether we are wide awake or fast asleep.

The most common instance that comes to mind is the forever awakened state of consciousness of a new parent. If you're actually a new parent as you're reading this—well, that's just good old synchronicity at work again—congratulations! But, need I say more to the brand-new parent? No, because I'm sure you've been on the phone with your friends or your mother, telling them that you don't know what it is to have a good night's sleep anymore. Even if your baby is sleeping through the night, your mind always seems to be on alert, waiting for when your child may need you.

A new parent isn't on alert in a negative sense (like waiting for the other shoe to drop), but rather in a paternal sense, and that's a sense that will never leave you once you become a parent. I believe the universe set it up that way from the beginning of time. It's the natural job of parents to be on standby for whenever their child needs a hug, a bath, a bottle, or a diaper change.

Even if you're not a parent, I'm sure you can visualize the state of mind I'm speaking of. You can be a parent of a new puppy or kitten and love your pet with the same kind of love some people have for their children. I know that my daughter Jackie has that kind of love for her dogs, Buster and Brandy. I cannot tell you how many nights she's woken up feeling one of them needed her, only to find that they did, just as a child needs a mother's attention. Jackie can tell from the way she hears her dogs plop down on the rug after a long day in the yard whether one of them is a little sad. If she hears Brandy sit down slowly, she knows that she must be having a problem with her hip, even though the dog can't tell her that. What Jackie has learned to do with the help of her dog-children is listen and observe their every move.

And you too can be listening with one ear open (a phrase my mother taught me when I had my first child), in the middle of the night, for any new whines or whimpers your new companion may be making. The parent in you tries to soothe your loving pet the same way the parent of a child wants to help her baby.

If you are a parent with older children, I'm sure you can recall when your baby was first born. Even when our children are grown, some of us never allow our consciousness to go into the deep REM state of sleep we enjoyed before our children came along. But just the same, we wouldn't change a thing.

Here's a workplace example of how your instincts can work with your senses and your observational skills.

Picture yourself at your desk, working diligently on a project or report that's due the following day. Being the ever-competent employee, you got up early and went into work before anyone else did just to get a jump on things before the office became noisy with chatter. Since the crack of dawn, you've been glued to your computer screen.

Then, suddenly, you hear footsteps approaching down the hallway. Automatically, your mind observes two things. First, your mind registers the familiar scent of someone who's walking in. The scent could be a recognizable hairspray, cologne, or perfume. That scent tells your consciousness exactly who it is walking down the corridor.

Now, take just a moment to think about how much you truly observed without ever raising your head from your computer screen. You could tell a lot about the person who was walking into the office, but that individual was doing more than just entering your office—the person was walking into your personal universe.

The second thing I'd like you to observe is the sound of the person's footsteps. Observe footsteps? Does the idea of observing footsteps sound odd to you? That's because we're not used to thinking of our sense of hearing as an observational wisdom. But when we're listening or hearing something, I believe that sense is one and the same as the sense of observing, because it's impossible to hear without observing.

You can hear from the pounding sound of the footsteps walking into the office that the person must be in a bad or anxious mood. Just by observing with your ears, you take in the sound of each heavy step, which to me as an intuitive, symbolizes someone dreading the day ahead.

So, even before you've turned away from your computer screen you can sense that you should steer clear of this co-worker today as much as possible. He's carrying with him, in every step, a negative energy field. And that negativity can endanger the course of your day, and possibly the success of the project you're working on.

You observed and calculated who was coming and what the outcome would have been, without any verbal communication with anyone. All your correct, innate calculations were done by observing your senses and listening to your instincts. You did all this without once looking up from your computer.

You see, your collective unconscious—a consciousness shared by the universe—was aware of the person's identity because of the familiar scent that was registered in your sensory memory bank. Our instincts register everyone we're familiar with, including their scent, their footsteps, and even the feel of a person's energy, be it positive or negative.

So you see, you don't have to have 20/20 vision, or your eyes wide open, in order to observe the universe and what your consciousness holds. And the universe embraces and marvels that your logical intellect has yet to be totally understood. I have no doubt that once you've acquired your seven keys and you become more aware of your conscious and subconscious psyche, you'll finally be able to imagine the new wonders your life will behold.

And the preceding chapters have already heightened your instincts so that you'll be able to answer your own life questions just using those instincts. But, just in case you need a little refresher course in observing your instincts, Key 6—"O" will get you there. So, if you're ready, let's begin our lesson in observing the universe with all our senses.

Lesson in Key 6—Observe

Most of us make our first mistake of the day the minute we open our eyes in the morning. How? We open them when our alarm clock goes off or when sunlight shines through the bedroom window. Or we may be awakened by thunder and the sound of rain pelting the side of our house. But when we're trying to enhance and improve the our instincts I've found it extremely helpful to prepare to awaken them the night before, the same way you would study for an exam you're taking the next day.

I propose that you make a conscious note to yourself, before you go to sleep, that before you open your eyes the next morning you will observe the universe with your eyes wide shut.

When you first awaken, remember to keep your eyes closed and allow your mind to be the only thing open to the universe. Then, if only for a moment or two, with your eyes still closed, take a virtual roll call of your five senses. For this exercise we're saving our sight sense for last.

The Five Classical Senses

1. **Touch:** Before you get out of bed, feel the blanket or sheet that covers you. Observe through your sense of touch the feeling of the fabric. Does it feel crisp and clean or is it time to change your bedding?

2. **Hearing:** Listen to the sounds that are coming from both inside and outside your home. If you have children or a roommate or a pet, are they up and about? Exercise your sense of hearing by observing the weather without opening your eyes. Does it sound like good weather out there? You can sense good or bad weather with your eyes shut. Listen to the wind. Are the trees swaying? If leaves are rustling and they sound a little quick or rough to you, nature is telling you that you might need a sweater or a jacket when you go outside. Do you hear rain hitting the side of the house or your windows? If so, then make a

mental note to take an umbrella with you when you leave the house.

3. **Taste:** Run your tongue against your teeth and taste what's going on inside your mouth. You can tell a lot about your body—not just your morning breath—by simply swallowing and exercising your taste buds first thing in the morning. Ask yourself if your sense of taste seems irregular this morning. If it does, then swallow and see how your throat feels. You may have a postnasal drip or you could be coming down with a sore throat if your taste buds are sour. If that's the case, you'll be able to take the proper precautions before you leave the house. All by simply examining and observing your sense of taste before emerging from your bedcovers.

4. **Smell:** Again before you open your eyes, inhale and observe through your sense of smell. Your instincts will pick up a few things. As you breathe in, examine instinctively. If there are odors, where are they coming from? Can you smell the coffee brewing in your next door neighbor's apartment? Next, ask yourself if you smell any rain or dampness in the air. Inhale again and ask yourself if you smell the lilac bush outside your window or other flowers in bloom?

Do you smell cologne, hair spray, baby powder or anything else in your bedroom? Exercise and observe your sense of smell and make a mental note to appreciate everything your instincts and consciousness are experiencing.

THE SENSE WITHOUT A NUMBER—MOOD SENSORY

Before we go on to review the last of our five senses, sight, I'd like to take you through just one more extremely important sensory observation that's not on our list of the first five senses. I like to call it our seventh sense—our mood sense or emotional sense. (The sixth sense is your intuition about your own life and those around you.)

What is a sensory mood? Sensory mood or a seventh sense is not something I read about somewhere or was taught by anyone. This is something I've learned myself through my years of reading consciousness. I've given it this name because I realized that as I was exercising and enhancing my natural instincts, I still felt as if I was missing an exercise somewhere in my being. It took me a while to figure out that what I needed to exercise and observe was my emotional or mood sense. I exercise it now routinely, especially when my life gets a little out of order. In hindsight, I realize when I had an off or bad day, it was usually because I didn't check my mood before I left my home.

So now I'm going to teach you what I've found to be one of the best lessons the universe has taught me. That's to check your emotional and psychological state of mind before you get out of bed in the morning.

Sound strange? Maybe, but I can tell you that this is an exercise that Jacqueline and I do every morning. It helps us comprehend what kind of state of consciousness we're beginning our day with. Once we've observed our mood, we can change it if we choose to.

You see, we are the masters—not only of our universe—but of our minds and moods. And you can essentially change what may very well be a nasty day to a brilliant, wondrous day, all because you've observed and adjusted something that it's in your power to change, and that's your attitude. You've heard of someone sometimes needing an attitude adjustment. Well, sometimes that someone's attitude is our own. We can fine-tune and enhance our frame of mind before we leave our bedroom with this simple exercise.

EXERCISING YOUR SEVENTH SENSE—MOOD SENSE

Remember that you're still in bed with your eyes closed. Now, sense what kind of mood or attitude you're awakening with. How do we sense our mood before our day begins and before we've even gotten out of bed? Simply by observing the energy of our body and our mind, and then beginning to feel the energy of our body. Are you waking up still feeling very tired?

If so, then shake off that tired feeling and get up as quickly as possible. Get yourself into a shower or a bath and get ready for your day, with gratitude that you're able to get up from your bed. Get up with gratitude that you have a warm bed to come home to. Get up with gratitude that you have a job to go to or a family to take care of.

And after you've thanked the universe for the miracle of yet another day on this physical plane, then promise yourself that you'll get to bed earlier this evening. As for today, you are not going to be a grouch or grumpy to anyone just because you're tired. Now is the time to rewire your thought process and think grateful and happy thoughts. When we become accustomed to feeling grateful for our life, it's hard to be grumpy or have a nasty attitude.

(This energy exercise applies only to anyone who doesn't have a medical reason as to why they're tired.)

5. **Sight:** Now that you've awakened your other senses and instincts to a satisfactory vibratory level, open your eyes slowly. Sit up in bed and plant your two feet solidly on the floor. As you're doing so, think how happy you are to be alive and conscious of everything around you. You are now

not just a piece of a puzzle. You're a beautifully completed puzzle ready for framing.

Take a good look around your room and observe what your other senses told you. Have some fun with the sensory exercise and see how accurate your other four senses were. Make a mental checklist of what your sensory observations were. Begin with your first exercise and see if your mental visualizations match up with the actual events taking place. For instance, look at your bedding and see if your touch sense was correct with its analysis. Does your bedding need to be changed or can it stay fresh for another day?

Now, get up from your bed and take a look out your window. What do you see? Is it raining or sunny? Are your flowers in bloom or do the garbage pails need to be emptied?

Look at your face in the mirror and smile. Look not just at your face's reflection, but at what you can tell about yourself by observing your image. Do you look like you had a good night's sleep or are there bags and dark circles under your eyes? When we pay attention to our senses, they will tell us what's going on within our bodies, if only we listen.

Create your day!

Now I'd like you to imagine yourself having a splendid day. In your mind's eye, create the day you wish to have. Try to envision yourself outside your body and looking at yourself in the future, even if the future is only two hours away. Create the day. Observe the day you're about to be part of. See yourself feeling well and looking great. See your entire day running like clockwork, without any negative blocks or attitudes getting in your way. When we observe our future, we become our future.

Last but not least, whether you work from home or commute to an office, or even if you're a stay-at-home parent or person, there is one final observation exercise that is very important for you to learn. That's the exercise of observing the people you spend your days with, be it at home or at work.

I don't want you to just look at them. I'd like you to observe them through the eyes of the universe and the eyes of collective unconsciousness. We are all one and we all can help each other, so I believe it's part of our job as human beings to try to be helpful and observant of people that are in our inner circle of life—those we see every day. Don't just look at their faces. Look at the colors of their complexions. We are not looking at ethnic backgrounds, but we're looking for signs of a healthy body or an ill one. I believe that when you become accustomed to utilizing your instincts, it becomes much simpler for you to actually receive medical intuition from your instincts.

One other huge gift that owning the key to observing the universe brings with it is the gift to change your destiny. When you follow your awakened instincts you can cut off negative outcomes at the pass.

Here's an instance: Let's say your boss comes into work looking flushed and sweaty. Normally, you really don't observe her face because you're busy catching up with your own work and your boss is just kind of there. But today, you notice that she's looking as though she's gone three rounds in a ring with Muhammad Ali and it's not quite 10 a.m.

On this occasion here's a mental note you should make to yourself: Don't bother the boss with unimportant or whiny issues, because if you do, you may get fired or chewed out like never before. Observe and you can hold on to your job. Observe and you can get the bonus you've been working so hard for. Observe and you can become the boss!

Telepathy

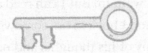

KEY 7

*It is thought and feeling which guides the universe,
not deeds.*

—EDGAR CAYCE

Have you ever wished you could read someone's mind? Of course
you have, everyone has. It's not impossible. The fact is we do it
all the time but we're not aware of it. We receive information
telepathically every day from everywhere in the universe, and we
usually just let it go in and out of our consciousness without paying it any mind.

Well, you can stop doing that now that you've learned how to
hone into your instincts and your first five senses. Mental telepathy

is defined as communication through means other than our normal five senses, or thought or energy transference. Scientists have already come to the conclusion that thoughts are a type of energy, and what I do is read energy. And if I can do it, then you can do it. I don't claim to read every word a person has on his mind, and in all honesty, I wouldn't want to. But I can read and sense accurately the emotions of a person I hone in on, somewhat like a laser beam, and I can pick up many of his thoughts and needs.

If I Could Read Your Mind, What Tales Would Your Thoughts Tell?

You'll find that once you've practiced exercising the first six keys, F, E, A, R, N, and O, finding and using Key 7 will come to you naturally. You've enhanced your instincts to the max, and you'll find that you'll be sensing and feeling things about people that you never did before.

Imagine going for a job interview and knowing just what the interviewer will be looking for in a new employee. It's not only possible, it's doable. I've done it on more than one occasion and so have many other people, though they're not always aware they were telepathically linked to their potential employer.

Mothers use telepathy all the time with their children, though we don't usually call it that. We call it mother's intuition, but it's more than that. It is much more than an instinct. It's actual thought communication between mother and child or parent and child.

This is one key that my daughter wishes I would lose every now and then, especially when she doesn't want me to know something. But alas, our telepathy isn't going anywhere because she's got it too. We've both learned that we must not invade each other's privacy by reading each other telepathically when we don't want to be read.

Why is telepathy more common with parents and children than with anyone else? Was your first answer going to be because of DNA? Nope. DNA has nothing to do with telepathy as I see it. Being related is an extra added bonus, but it's not the only reason why parents and children or family members can feel what their loved ones are going through at certain moments.

The telepathic communication described below occurred between my granddaughter Charlotte Rose and myself when she was just fourteen months old.

One morning right before I was about to awaken I had a dream. I thought that my granddaughter was speaking to me, very clearly telling me how much she loved the clowns and the waterfalls. And that she wanted mommy to get the little grey kitten. (At only fourteen months, I knew Charlotte couldn't speak to me as clearly as she was conversing with me in my dream-state.)

A few minutes later I woke myself up because the dream felt so real to me. I wanted to see if it was just a dream or if I was picking up on her consciousness through telepathy.

I figured if she was telepathically speaking to me, I didn't have to be asleep to hear her. So I sat up in my bed and turned on the television, just to have some background noise and to see if I could get the dream conversation out of my head. (I knew that if it was telepathic communication it would continue whether I was awake or sleeping.)

Charlotte's communication stopped for a few minutes as I watched the morning news, then suddenly it began again. I was hearing the same thing over again—how much she loved the clowns and the waterfalls, and something about getting a new grey kitten.

But now, while I was awake, I was also seeing Charlotte sleeping in her crib, wearing pink polka-dot pajamas. Since telepathy had never happened between me and any of my grandchildren before, I couldn't wait to learn more. Was Charlotte speaking to me telepathically or was I just being my psychic self? I called my daughter-in-law Angela, Charlotte's mom, and told her what was going on in my head. There was silence for a moment and then Angela spoke, sounding a little apprehensive. Angela said Charlotte hadn't slept well the night before so she had put on my children's meditation tape for her to listen to and help soothe her. (Okay, now I knew how my granddaughter connected to my energy—she was listening to my voice and then she zoned in on the real me.) Angela went on to say that they had watched a new TV program while they were on vacation in Canada and it was all about clowns. Charlotte loved it. Then she told me they had gone to see the Falls while they were there. (I had known they were going to Canada on vacation but I had no idea exactly where they were going or what they'd be doing while there.) But the thing that made my daughter-in-law shake in her boots a little was the mention of the grey kitten.

The afternoon before, Angela received a call from her sister asking her if she wanted a grey kitten that she had found. I asked her where Charlotte was when this conversation took place, and she said, "She was on my lap, but I didn't think she would understand."

So what is my conclusion? Charlotte absolutely transmitted telepathically the information she wanted to express but couldn't because of her very new verbal communication skills. And she transmitted those thoughts to the person who was speaking to her through the meditation CD while she was in a REM state.

Before you go thinking, "Of course you can communicate with your granddaughter, you're telepathic," I promise you that it's not the only reason why we communicated. It's true that I've been telepathic ever since I can remember, but when

I became confused and ill, I lost my focus in life because of my fears for my future. Then, my telepathy was nowhere to be found.

Fortunately, I found it again with the help of my daughter Jacqueline, who made me remember who I was when I was fearless. I credit prayer and meditation as the guiding forces that allowed me to heal, focus, and float back to the confident, intuitively awakened me. And once my intuition and instincts were up to par, I was guided to write down my lessons. They are the seven keys that I used to enhance my instincts to a higher energy level, higher than they ever were before.

Although you may not become a professional intuitive by using the seven keys, I have no doubt that your instincts will become sharper and clearer. You'll find yourself picking up people's thoughts without even trying, which I must honestly admit isn't always a great thing. I mean, think about it. If someone doesn't like you or if someone tells you that you look lovely but you're telepathically hearing the exact opposite of what they're saying, you sometimes want to shut it off. But don't. It's better to know the truth and where you stand with a person. I like to think of times like those as bitter pills. They're hard to swallow, but in the end, they make you well, so you're better off when you take them.

And you'll always be better off and enhance your life to heights you haven't even imagined once you learn how to telepathically communicate with not only your loved ones, but with anyone you choose, including your four-legged friends.

Seven Steps to Telepathic Communication

1. First, believe that you *can* communicate. Get comfortable and relax. Then practice with your family or friends, using a deck of playing cards or index cards that you've written something on such as simple yet visual words like cat or car. Look at the cards and then have the person sitting across from you—or you can even do it over the phone—try to guess what you're reading or thinking.

2. Stay focused at all times and meditate before you begin to transmit any information to a second party.

3. Visualize sending your thoughts to someone on a laser beam of light. Remember telepathy is accessed by energy and light is energy.

4. Visualize your thoughts blending in with the energy of the person you're trying to communicate with. In other words, think of it as the melding of the minds to become one.

5. Instead of sending a message, try asking a question and see what response or responses you receive back.

6. Remember, your energy must remain fully charged at all

times during your mental transmission. So get psyched and
stay psyched.

7. If at first you don't receive any telepathic verbal communication, don't think that you've failed. It's very common that
you'll receive emotional communication your first few tries.
You may get a message or a sense about how the person is
feeling, either mentally or physically or both.

The Knowledge and Study of Your Chakras

There are seven spiritual bodies associated with consciousness.
They correspond to seven chakras, or energy centers, located
along the center of the body. They also correspond with seven
spiritual planes that are accessed in different states of consciousness.

We're going to learn how to exercise your chakras, but before we do, let me explain the significance of chakras and exactly
what they are. Then, we can go forward and balance and exercise
them.

Chakra is a Sanskrit term meaning wheel or circle. It expresses
the life-force energy in our body and refers to a spinning sphere
of biogenetic activity from major nerves from the spinal column.
It defines different nerves within the body. Chakras are also sometimes referred to as the wheel of life.

The most commonly known chakras are the seven I will talk about here. They ascend from the base of our spine to the top of our head. Each chakra is associated with a certain color and aspect of consciousness as well as with other characteristics of our being.

Picture your body standing still, with the colors of your aura spinning around you—like a spinning wheel. The spinning is produced by your energy. Your chakras are connected to all your senses, including sound, light, and color.

When even one of our chakras is out of balance, our formerly stable body is now unbalanced from the inside out. I believe it's necessary for adults to understand about their invisible chakras, but it's also very important for us to teach our children about their chakras. They can learn from their early years how to keep balanced from the inside out. And, parents or grandparents, teaching yourself and your children about maintaining your chakras is far from an ordeal. Once you realize how easy it is to do, you can have fun with it while helping each other. Maintaining and enhancing your chakras isn't just for people who practice yoga, study Buddhism, or take karate. And, remember we are never too young or too old to learn how to help ourselves and others around us.

The Location of Your Seven Chakras

Chakras are said to have an extrasensory function, playing a part in instinctive responses. These are sometimes viewed as extending only out to the skin of the body, but are often thought to extend to the boundary of the aura.

1. Base of the spine/Name: Root
2. Lower abdomen/lower back (below navel)/Name: Sacral
3. Solar plexus (between the navel and base of sternum, which is the central vertical bone in the rib-cage)/Name: Solar
4. Heart (center of chest)/Name: Heart
5. Throat (base of neck)/Name: Throat
6. Brow (lower forehead, between eyes)/Name: Third eye
7. Crown (top of the head)/Name: Crown

The Colors of Chakras and How They Help Us

Before we begin to learn about the colors of our chakras, I'd like to first make you aware that color is extremely important and not to be taken lightly. Color itself is living energy, and the universe as well as our own bodies are only energy in vibration. So if your energy level is low and you feel like you're in the dumps, you can make yourself feel more energetic or less depressed just by exercising your chakras.

How can you do this? Very easily, by being aware of how you feel, by listening to your body, and by keeping each of your chakras centered and in alignment with your body and the universe. We can help keep centered and enhance whatever is ailing us by using certain colors of each chakra to awaken and energize each any part of our body and consciousness.

Our chakras also control the energies of the major and vital organs of our physical bodies.

This exercise in color healing, or exploring the colors of our chakras, has no age limit. I have found it useful for children, grandchildren, parents, and friends. Even if someone is too young to hold a crayon or can't color or paint because of their age or disability, their energy can be assisted just by placing certain colors in their line of vision. This, in turn, will help enhance and awaken their energy to a healthier and happier level.

So for those parents who don't know what to do with your children to get them out of a certain state of mind, take out a coloring book. Don't let your child just sit alone and color. Join in and direct her to use a certain color that you believe may need enhancing between the two of you. (If you have more than one child—and the more the merrier—I recommend having a set of crayons or markers or finger paints on hand for each child so they can use the same colors if they choose to.)

Now that we've covered the relationship between color and energy, we can go on to explaining the colors of our chakras.

1. RED

The first chakra, root, is red in color. The color red enhances and stimulates brain wave activity. It also can increase heart rate, respiration, and blood pressure.

If you've already been diagnosed by a physician with a weak heart or a murmur, asthma or low blood pressure, of course follow the instructions of your doctor, but I recommend you also use the color red as part of your natural healing process.

Tips for Healing Using Your Red Chakra

For instance, let's say your blood pressure is too high or too low, and you're already doing everything your doctor has suggested. You're taking the medications prescribed to normalize it, and making the recommend diet and lifestyle changes. I would go one step further: I would also wear the color red as much as possible, even if I could only wear a red colored tie to work every day.

The color red should also be incorporated in what your skin touches. So ladies and gents, as well as you kiddies, I'm pretty sure we all have at least one red T-shirt or sweatshirt in our closet.

If you don't, go out and buy an inexpensive undershirt or T-shirt and wear it whenever possible when you're not feeling up to par.

2. ORANGE

Our second chakra, sacral, is orange in color. It is the chakra of happiness and intelligence. Just thinking about the color orange makes me smile; it has always been my favorite color. Although the color orange is lovely to look at, the energy that it holds can also help stimulate your appetite. (And that's very likely the reason why I never suffered from loss of appetite as a child!)

Orange is a very emotional and sensitive color. I've spent many years asking people—family, friends, and clients alike—about their favorite color. I would suggest as part of your chakra exercise that you ask your family and friends to join the experiment. You should keep track of each other's favorite colors. Just tell them to exercise their observational skills and senses and remember what they see. Then as time goes by, see if you can be of help to them if any problems arise in their daily life. For example, imagine your child or family member, or even a friend, informs you that his appetite has been less than normal lately, and he's also been feeling a little nauseated, which could be because of the onset of a cold or flu. Perhaps they're feeling that way because of a chronic ailment that is now affecting their desire for food. Well, in cases such as these, knowing what chakra colors to introduce may be just what the doctor ordered. With your advice, their enhancement of a certain color will not only make them feel better but will enhance the color of their aura.

You also may notice that the most intuitive and supersensitive people just adore the colors orange, peach, or tangerine. Frank Sinatra was known to say that his favorite color was orange. I should say *is* orange because as you know, I don't believe in death—only the demise of the skeletal body. There is no death of the living conscious mind.

Tips for Healing Your Orange Chakra

If you've been feeling very anxious lately or if you've been having an extreme case of acid reflux or what Italians call agita, I recommend you wear the color orange as much as possible while you're experiencing digestive problems. If you have an orange or tangerine blanket and lay it across your stomach or your midsection when you're not feeling well, it will help naturally with your digestive system. (Of course, see your physician for any medical problems first. But as an intuitive explorer of consciousness, I cannot rule out enhancing your chakras to help yourself heal.)

In recent years I've noticed that more and more children have been diagnosed with acid reflux, and sometimes from infancy. With that in mind, and seeing that the color orange has been known to soothe the digestive system, evoke happiness, and stimulate appetites, I would make sure my children had many orange toys or stuffed animals around them so they can focus their color while they play.

Another little hint for moms or dads: if your children are fussy eaters, try putting their food on an orange plate and see how they respond. Lastly, for new parents whose children are having trouble sleeping because of colic or acid reflux, create an orange crib mobile. Simply cut some stars or other shapes out of orange paper or fabric and attach them with a string to an existing mobile. Make sure the string or cord is tied or glued securely to the mobile. And if your baby has a tummy ache even after you've given her the medications that the doctor has recommended, lay a clean, dry, orange washcloth or receiving blanket on her tummy as you sit her on your lap and talk calmly to her.

3. YELLOW

Our third chakra, solar, represents the solar plexus. It is said to energize our body, relieve depression, and improve memory and digestive problems. Solar, our yellow chakra, represents wisdom and connects us to mental health.

In my eyes, the color yellow always symbolizes sunshine, so I can naturally see how this chakra can help people who are depressed or just in a mental funk.

Tips for Healing Using Your Yellow Chakra

Since the color yellow can symbolize sunshine and positive energy, in order for us to try to help enhance someone out of a melancholy state, why not have them take a walk in the sunshine? Or, paint or color using yellow. It's a great idea to paint a family room or den a light yellow so everyone spending time in the room stays in a good mood.

The use of the color yellow, I believe, will help children and adults who have been diagnosed with attention deficit disorder (ADD), or attention deficit hyperactivity disorder (ADHD). Again, wearing the color yellow will also help enhance someone's mood and will help awaken their memory. If you have a grandmother or parent whose short-term memory isn't what it once was, buy them a nice cheerful yellow tablecloth for their kitchen table so they can see it and be brightened by it every day.

4. GREEN

Our fourth chakra, heart, is the color green. It can have a calming effect on the upper part of the body and has healing properties. Green also brings the chakras into alignment and balance, and can bring balance to the nervous system. Green is the color of growth and rejuvenation. You should avoid wearing the color green if you have any type of allergy or rash that you don't want to spread.

Tips for Healing Using Your Green Chakra

Although my favorite color out of all the chakra colors is orange, after I studied all the chakras and their colors and realized how they could be used to enhance healing, I smiled. Why? Because about three years ago, before I had done any intensive research on chakras and their healing colors, I had changed all the rugs in my home to sage green. I also had the walls of my living room and dining room painted a darker green.

And seeing that I have multiple sclerosis, a disease that attacks the nervous system, it's obvious why my instincts chose the color. It was to calm and balance my nervous system. I must admit I feel the most at peace in my Long Island home where the color green in incorporated throughout the house.

Green is a soothing color and can calm anxieties as well as relax your physical body. Spiritually, green is the color of love, and not just any type of love. It's the color of perfect love!

So ladies and gentlemen, if you're looking for love the next time you go on that first date, I'd recommend you choose a nice light green shirt or sweater. I'd go with sage green rather than a darker green if you want to create a loving and nurturing feeling to the date. Sage means wisdom, and the lighter the color the less stress we feel and the more at peace we become.

If you're already attached and you feel as though your love life could use a boost, then plan to wear something green on your next date night, or perhaps buy something cozy for you both, like matching sage green robes! (Some of you may be thinking that money is green, so why not just give my honey money? The answer is no, green money doesn't count—not when you're aiming for perfect love.)

5. BLUE

Our fifth chakra, throat, radiates with the color blue. Wearing or meditating on the color blue can help clear up sore throats and/or respiratory illness. Blue also has a calming effect on our minds and our will. The color blue, when concentrated on correctly, can help us make the correct decisions by inducing a sense of calm and life balance.

Tips for Healing Using Your Blue Chakra

If you find yourself waking up with a sore throat, the first thing to do, while you're still lying in bed, is to swallow again just to be sure your throat isn't just dry. When you do gulp and realize that your throat is in fact sore, close your eyes and take a minute or two to meditate.

In your meditation, I'd like to focus in your mind's eye on the color blue. Imagine yourself on a sailboat, drifting smoothly and safely in the blue waters off a tropical island. Now while you're still in your meditation visualization, I'd like you to lean out over the side of the boat and get a good view of the beautiful, serene blue ocean. Next, I'd like you to look up at the cloudless sky. Breathe in deep the smell of the cleansing salt water, at the same time breathing in the blue fresh air.

Is there anything in your imagination that looks and feels cooler and calmer, or more refreshing, than what you have just inhaled and envisioned? I can't think of any, but if you can, be my guest and imagine what you wish, as long as it's blue and calm.

Wearing blue also allows the effects of that color to penetrate a person's body as well as consciousness. Wearing blue can lower your blood pressure. Of course, if you have any chronic illness, always make it your business to get regular medical check-ups. Use our chakra healing as an additional natural therapy. Its a good idea, too, to maintain a low-salt diet and keep away from fast foods that have additives.

Lastly, to help alleviate any throat, respiratory, or blood pressure issues you may have, take a walk outside when you can. If you can't take a walk, then sit outside when weather permits and just gaze at the beautiful sunlight and blue sky. Take a dip in a pool, if one is available to you. You don't even have to go in the water if you don't want to. Just sit by the aqua-blue water and you'll feel better within minutes.

6. INDIGO

Our sixth chakra, brow, also known as our third eye, is the color indigo. Indigo is a hue between blue and violet. It has magnificent healing properties for anyone with an autoimmune disease such as lupus, arthritis, thyroid disease, HIV/AIDS, and diabetes. Some find indigo color helpful in healing specific facial problems such as skin blemishes or sinus problems. Of all the chakras, indigo is known as the most prevailing color of intuition. And when we're connected to our intuition, we're more easily able to tap into our unconscious self as well as our conscious self, and heal more effectively.

Tips for Healing Using Your Indigo Chakra

Some chakras are sites or centers of the psychic faculties. Our indigo chakra, brow, is one of them. Because indigo is a combination of blue and violet, I believe it's safe to say that utilizing this color when trying to heal any part of the body might be much simpler than using the other chakra colors.

It may be a little difficult to find fabric in a pure indigo color. I recommend that you mix the two colors—blue and violet—onto a piece of white cotton (like tie-dying). Or if you're lucky, you'll be able to go on the Web and find something in the indigo color. My recommendation is to meditate on the color and see it going into each and every organ that may be affected by an autoimmune problem. Since brow, or the sixth chakra, is the most intuitive of chakras, intense meditation with the color should be very helpful to your healing.

If your problems lie with your sinuses or face, place an indigo-colored cloth on your face while in a meditative state and ask your consciousness to help you heal from the inside out.

7. VIOLET

Last but not least in our stunning spectrum of healing colors is the seventh chakra, crown, represented by the beautiful color of violet. Known to provide a peaceful environment when utilized in the home and when worn on the body, it's also helpful when the color itself touches your skin. It can boost your immune system and has been used since ancient times as a remedy for headaches and migraines. The color violet is also defined as the color of strength.

Tips for Healing Using Your Violet Chakra

Violet, the color of our seventh chakra, is my first choice for the color of a child's playroom, be it for a boy or girl. Why? Because the color invokes peace and harmony, and every household needs more of that!

As for healing with the color violet, my recommendations are the same as for the other colors. Wear the color if you have a headache or if you feel as though you're catching a cold or a flu bug. But I'd suggest going one step further: keep some actual live violet plants or flowers in your home whenever these medical issues arise. In fact, these plants and flowers are so beautiful that I wouldn't wait until I was getting sick to bring them into my home or workplace.

Chakra Outcome

To keep all your chakras balanced properly, you should practice using these seven colors with meditation therapy whenever possible. After a while, you'll find you're using them all the time unconsciously as a regular routine.

The best tip I can give you with regard to having all your chakras protected and enhanced at all times is to make or buy a bed quilt with the seven chakra colors on it. If can't find an appropriate quilt, go to your local fabric store and buy half a yard of each color. You can sew them together by hand or with a sewing machine, or you can use sewing glue. We'll call this your chakra patch quilt.

I think once you see how well it works for you, you'll be making one for everyone you know. It would make a great baby shower gift or a birthday gift, too. After all, what better gift is there to give to anyone than the gift of health and wellness that comes directly from you, so you can help heal a person from the inside out!

Symptoms of Chihuahua Energy

Earlier, when we were learning how to relax your energy and how to master your fourth key, we introduced the term Chihuahua energy: that nervous, anxious, insecure, obsessive aura seen in some people (and yes, in those small dogs, too). It can take over your clear, seeing instincts and interfere with your ability to observe and use your other keys.

Having Chihuahua energy is also detrimental to the relationships you have with people all around you. We can get this monkey—or Chihuahua—off your back for good.

Jacqueline and I have learned how to rid ourselves of this energy, and stop ourselves from ever again catching the Chihuahua germ, by getting rid of the drama in our lives. Jacqueline has come home so many nights after going out with her friends and told me about how silly or anxious some of her girlfriends act around certain people—usually boys. Jackie has said, "Mom, you should have seen how many times this girl we were out with called her boyfriend on his cell phone just to make sure he was where he said he was going to be because she didn't trust him." My reply to Jackie, "She's a Chihuahua!"

Jackie and I have learned so much just by observing other people's Chihuahua energy, so now Jackie knows how not to act or to react when it comes to dating or to everyday life. And, I thank God and the universe that she's learned this lesson at such an early age, so she can help not only herself but her friends who seem to crave the drama in their lives.

No Drama, Please

I've found that most people who are carrying the Chihuahua anxiousness have quite a bit of drama in their lives. In fact, some of them thrive on it and have gotten so used to their soap-opera type of life that being calm and centered feels somewhat unnatural to them.

And as an intuitive who has been listening to and guiding people from all over the globe for over thirty years, I've found that most of the questions I am asked by clients—especially those who have lived drama-filled lives—are about how they can get their lives back on track. They want to know how I can direct them toward a more peaceful, fulfilling, purposeful life. We all have some level of drama: we are surrounded by conflict or conflicted people who seem to thrive on arguments and negative situations. But those Chihuahuas out there have more drama than anything else.

You know the type of person I'm talking about. We've all encountered a few individuals in our lifetime whose conversations always seem to start with a negative situation they've just experienced, and it's always someone else's fault. They are what I call drama magnets. DMs don't seem to be happy or have anything to talk about unless it concerns an argument they've just had, or a fight they'd like to have with an ex-husband, boyfriend, girlfriend, in-law . . . Well, you get the idea. But to pinpoint the definition even more: the DMs want a dispute with anyone who doesn't think exactly the way they do about anything. And when I say anything, I mean anything. Drama magnets will look to find conflict with another individual over the weather.

When such an individual seeks my counsel, and tells me she's come to me to find the peace of mind she wants, I often know she's kidding herself. I can consciously read that she really isn't seeking peace, she just wants my approval of the way she conduct her life. DMs want me to tell them that I agree with how ridiculous everyone else in their life is. My reply to them is this: "Aren't you sick of all the drama in your life already?"

Please don't think I'm uncaring when I ask a person this question because that's the last thing I want to be. The time I have to spend on each person is limited, and I don't want to waste precious moments looking for easy or politically correct ways to tell them that they're the ones who are making their lives crazy, or at least that they're partially at fault.

Every now and then we all need someone to tell us to stop the lunacy that has become our life and abnormal reality. Ah, now you may be thinking, who is she to say what's normal or abnormal? She's not a doctor or therapist. I am a medical intuitive and I do use my intuition in this capacity on a daily basis, but I do not prescribe medication. I recommend what doctors people should see and how they should listen to certain physicians. I do what they ask me to do—I read their energy as an IEC (intuitive explorer of consciousness) and I don't believe in wasting time. Time is just too valuable. My hope is for them to quickly see what I'm seeing by the use of telepathy and through my explanation. I do explain step-by-step everything I'm seeing and sensing with the hope that the person I am teaching or directing will be able to read his or her own energy next time and see how to make the correct turns in the journey of life, rather than get lost again and not ask for directions.

Let's get rid of your drama. See when and where the drama began and don't try to judge who did what to whom first—just look and observe and see where you could erase some of the daily drama that has been absorbing your good chi (energy). When you leave the grudges behind and allow the drama to be removed from your life and energy source, you'll find that within days your life will begin to change for the better. And there's one definite rule you must observe when ridding yourself of all the unnecessary drama in your life: you must rid yourself of all those who refuse to help themselves get off their drama merry-go-round.

Once you've taken a good look at yourself and the drama, you can help yourself and the people around you to find peace and harmony in your lives. But you cannot allow yourself to fall back into your old routine of arguing back at them or having negative or nasty answers waiting in the wings of your conversation. This is something you can change overnight and is not difficult at all, not after you've seen and realized that negative drama only brings bad karma to you, and that karma will affect every aspect of your life negatively.

Are You a Chihuahua?

So this talk of drama hits home a little, but you're not sure you're a full-fledged Chihuahua? Maybe, and maybe not. Keep reading and see if anything else hits home.

CHIHUAHUA SYMPTOMS FOR SINGLES

If you're in the world of dating but you find you're not having success, you may have too much in common with those little nervous dogs. Take a look at your dating relationships and see if you have any of these symptoms. If so, you might be in the market for a Chihuahua leash.

1. You're worried that she is dating someone else the entire time you're dating her.
2. You're obsessed and anxious awaiting his phone calls or emails.
3. If the person you're dating doesn't call you in what you believe is the appropriate time for someone who's exclusive with you, you start asking your friends and anyone else who will listen for their opinion on why you haven't received any communications.
4. You stop dating other people before you have mutually agreed on a committed relationship.
5. You're imagining yourself living with the new person you're dating after only knowing her for three weeks.
6. You're constantly worried that your new girlfriend is still cordial to her ex.
7. You're analyzing every detail of your date when it's over,

with the intention of deciphering any negative signals or comments you may have overlooked during your time to-gether.

If you've answered yes to four out of the seven questions, call the dogcatcher. There's no doubt in my mind you're a Chihuahua. But have no fear. All is not lost, because once you realize you have the symptoms, there's an antidote.

The Outcome

If you ignore the symptoms, they're not going to go away on their own, and there's no good future for a relationship that involves a partner with Chihuahua energy.

If you've answered the questions and logically you know that you match more of the questions then you'd like, but you still don't believe that it's necessary for you to change your anxious ways, see what my statistics show.

Over the past year I've been keeping track—a poll of sorts—of return callers to my radio show who I believed to have Chihuahua tendencies. I kept track of this poll in my private journal. Here's what I found:

- 90 percent of the callers who called about relationship issues, and who I had specifically said had CE (Chihuahua energy), were not dating that same person about three months after their initial call.

- Of the 10 percent who were still dating the same person (by some miracle, I might add!), I've concluded that the person they were dating also had CE tendencies in their DNA.

Having an anxious relationship with your mate can also cause trouble for your friendships with other people. Two anxious Chihuahua couples may all get along just fine, but if you're a nervous couple, I can almost guarantee that you won't be able to maintain a relationship with another couple whose relationship is calm and relaxed. And if the anxious couple decides to procreate, they'll be giving birth to little CEs! Why? Because as Deepak Chopra says: What you see, you shall become!

In addition, I've come to observe that children who have one or more parent with the CE factor are children who are very likely to wind up with baby acid reflux, and they're usually on medication for the problem when they're only weeks old.

So if you believe you have any of the aforementioned tendencies or symptoms, fix them before you get married and have children. Do you want your children to be raised by a calm mommy or daddy or by a small barking dog?

SYMPTOMS OF A MARRIED CHIHUAHUA

Simply walking down the aisle and saying "I do" isn't going to solve your Chihuahua energy. You may have gone into your marriage a little unsure of yourself and your insecurities have grown over the years. Or maybe more recent events have led to your Chihuahua behaviors. Do you recognize yourself here?

1. You're insecure about yourself and your marriage. You continuously ask your spouse at the most inappropriate times, "Do you really love me?" even though your spouse has done nothing to make you feel he's changed his love for you in any way.
2. You find a problem with your spouse's family member when no one's actually done anything wrong to hurt you or to disrespect you.
3. You're continuously checking your spouse's cell phone for damaging hidden information, as if she has a lover hidden on the side.
4. If you're a female Chihuahua, you make your husband go to the mall with you because you don't trust him home alone or out doing anything without you. If you're a male Chihuahua, you're so insecure that you take the car keys from your wife's purse so she can't go anywhere without you. (Insecurity and jealousy affect both sexes.)

5. The pathetic looking guy in the chair outside the woman's dressing room holding his wife's purse? You know him. He's married to a Chihuahua and he's allowing her to own his chi (energy). That is, if he'd really rather not be there. If he does, then he's just a nice guy.

6. A Chihuahua wife forces her husband to take her children everywhere he goes. Not so he can bond with his children, but so that the children can keep an eye on him. (Again, this is done with no real suspicions other than her own insecurities.)

7. A Chihuahua wife or husband feels threatened by silence. They must have a conversation every minute when they are home with their spouse. Silence to them means they're not loved. I'm not talking about communication, which is a necessity in any relationship. Even if you're married, you sometimes need your space and your quiet time and Chihuahuas won't let their spouses have it—or at least not without an argument. You see, if you're arguing, you're not silent, so either way, the Chihuahua wins.

8. A Chihuahua mate believes that her spouse might also be silent because he is guilty of something or because he's thinking of someone else.

If you saw yourself in three out of eight symptoms, then I'm shocked that you're still married! And if you are, I'm shocked you're still sharing the same bedroom! But three out of eight isn't all that bad. It tells me there's room for growth and you haven't beaten your marriage to death yet for no good reason.

If you've answered yes to all the above, call a doctor, a psychologist or psychiatrist—and then a lawyer.

I know you may think I'm making light of your heartache or that I'm trying to come off like a comedian, but I'm dead serious. With today's divorce rate skyrocketing to 50 percent, and half of all marriages ending in less than five years, I can appreciate the fear and the reasoning behind some people feeling anxious and nervous that their marriage will end horribly. But I want this lesson to teach you that everyone needs their space and everyone needs to be trusted. If you don't allow your spouse some room, she'll sooner or later find a way to get away from you, even for a little while. If you give her her space and you show her the trust she deserves, then you'll have her around you so much that you'll be the one asking for some time for yourself.

You see, we get married because we love the person and we don't want to be with anyone else mentally or physically for the rest of our lives. But that doesn't mean we can't have friends and spend time with them innocently. (This goes for husbands as well as wives.)

Once your instincts are totally awakened, you won't have to worry at all about making the right choices about who you should marry, or if your husband or wife is cheating, and you won't be insecure and want to own them instead of LOVE them. With your instincts awakened you will enhance your marriage to where you'll feel lucky to be in love every single day. But it also works for you the other way also. With your instincts awake you can feel when the tides are turning in your marriage, and you can correct them immediately. Or you'll be able to tell whether you married the right person or the wrong person. With knowledge comes choices, but we should never obsess or allow our marriage to make us ill. With your instincts awakened, that never will happen.

Conclusion:
Keep the Journey
Going

Now that you are equipped with the tools and keys to open any doorway you choose to enhance every aspect of your life, I, too, feel complete. I thank you for making me brush up on my instincts once again by writing this book. I also am extremely grateful for the privilege of entering your consciousness and I hope that your journey of enhancement will be as uplifting and life altering as was my daughter's and mine.

The very last thing I want to add to this life-enhancing book on how to awaken your instincts is the powerful brilliance that prayer and a positive attitude can bring to your life and to the lives of all those you encounter.

While you're in the midst of enhancing every aspect of your

life and awakening your instincts I recommend that you develop a better and deeper spiritual connection with the Divine. Make it your business to pray every day as a form of meditation and gratitude for the life you now hold so dearly to your heart. A life you love so much that you want to enhance it to the max and you'll do whatever it takes to get you to the highest vibratory level possible.

For those who choose not to pray, then find a poem or a mantra that touches your heart and soul and recite it daily while giving thanks for all you've accomplished and for the miracles that are on their way to you.

In the meantime, Jacqueline and I thank you for becoming part of our collective unconscious universe and taking time out of your very busy lives to read our guidepoints and our life lessons. We hope you find them as useful in your lives as we have found them in ours.

We are greatly honored to be a small part of your life's journey and we bid you peace, joy, and all the things you wish for yourself times three.

Many blessings to you and yours!

Ciao Bellas!

Acknowledgments

For my sons, and Jacqueline's brothers, Chris and Carl Corry, thank you both for being the men in our lives! And of course thank you to their wives, Angela and Jeannine, for being part of our wonderful family and for sharing your husbands with us.

For our little additions, my grandchildren and Jacqueline's nephews and nieces—Taylor, Tommy, Danny, CJ, Charlotte Rose, and our littlest angel Catherine Grace—our lives are awakened even more every time we are in your presence.

For my parents and Jacqueline's grandparents, Michael and Anna Saliba. Without your inspiration and love none of this would have been possible.

For James and Mary Sullivan, Jacqueline's grandparents in heaven whom we both loved dearly and whose presence we feel often. And lastly, for Jacqueline's father, Dennis Sullivan, whose wit and good humor is only surpassed by his compassion for the American Veterans. Without Dennis there would be no Jacqueline.

Thank you to my dearest friend, Christine Dumas, for the long hours she spent sitting by the phone as I read each chapter to her in the wee hours of the morning. And thank you to Johanna Castillo who awakened the writer in me and the mother in herself.